QUIZ BOOK

FOR GROUPS

Famous People

Ted Payne
Edited by Robin Dynes

Speechmark Publishing Ltd
Telford Road, Bicester, Oxon OX26 4LQ, UK

Coventry University

Published by
Speechmark Publishing Ltd, Telford Road, Bicester, Oxon OX26 4LQ,
United Kingdom.
Telephone: +44 (0) 1869 244 644 Fax: +44 (0) 1869 320 040
www.speechmark.net

002-3104/Printed in the United Kingdom/1010

British Library Cataloguing in Publication Data
Payne, Ted
   Quiz book for groups : famous people
   1. Questions and answers
   I. Title   II. Dynes, Robin
   793.7'3

ISBN 0 86388 524 1
(Previously published by Winslow Press Ltd under ISBN 0 86388 158 0)

Contents

Section 1

Section 2

Section 3

Section 4

Section 5

Section 6

Section 7

Section 8

Section 9

Section 10

Introduction

Who is this book for?

The popularity of quizzes has grown enormously since the Second World War. This was encouraged first on radio and then with the spread of television, on which quiz shows have been very successful. It has become clear that people enjoy both participating in and watching them. In more recent years quizzes have become regular entertainment in local village halls, pubs, social clubs and community centres. They provide a great deal of fun and enjoyment for participants and spectators alike.

This makes quizzes ideal material for anyone organizing group activities in any setting, be it a day centre, hospital, nursing home, community centre, education centre or in residential accommodation. Through the use of quizzes, individuals can be encouraged to interact with each other, share knowledge and experience, exercise memory skills, reminisce or gain new knowledge. All this and fun too!

What is in the book?

The book contains 50 quizzes – a total of 1000 questions – all of which are related to people: past, present and fictional. It is divided into 10 sections, each containing five different quizzes with 20 questions. Each section contains a quiz based on the surnames of famous people, a 'pot luck' quiz and three others on different subjects.

Using the book

The quizzes can be used in many different ways. Here are some suggestions:

- Put the questions to the whole group; anyone who knows the answers calls out.

- Each member of the group is asked a question in turn. If the person has difficulty answering, offer the question to the rest of the group.

- Divide the group into two or more teams, allowing team members to confer before answering.

- **Divide the group into teams. This time put questions to individual members in turn. If the person is unable to answer a question, it can be given to the whole team. (If a score is being kept, fewer points can be given when help is needed.)**

Teams do tend to generate more pace and excitement. However, not everyone may get to answer questions. If you ask each person individual questions, some people may feel threatened or put on the spot. Also the pace will be slower, but the entertainment will last longer. The least threatening format is to put the questions to the whole group without scoring.

You can, of course, mix the formats: have a round of questions in which teams call out the answers and then another with individuals answering, and so on. Whichever format you use, do make sure that everyone understands the ground rules, any points system changes at the beginning of each round, and any time limits imposed for answering.

The quizzes may be photocopied and given to each individual, or you can call out the questions and have each person write down their answers (note that the answers face the questions for ease of use).

Do bear in mind what your aims are when deciding the format for your group. If it is to aid interaction or for reminiscence it will be more productive to have answers called out when the questions are asked. This way the person responding can be encouraged to expand on the answer. They may say how they felt or feel about the personality, share their experience of seeing them in concert, and so on. Other members of the group can also contribute. This can also help to defuse any competitiveness that some people may feel is intimidating.

Striking a balance between giving people the opportunity to talk about the answers and keeping the quiz going is important. This helps ensure that no one is left out, is ignored, gets impatient or feels one or two individuals have all the limelight.

Some people respond with enthusiasm to competitiveness and others shrink away from it. You will need to judge which balance best suits your group. To encourage competitiveness, prizes can be introduced. If you do this, bear in mind that anyone who does not win a prize may be very disappointed, resentful or feel left out. It is a matter of judgement as to what will produce the best response from a particular group.

It is also important to remember that the questions asked should be about subjects or happenings that members of the group could reasonably be expected to know about, given their age, background and so on. This is particularly important when putting questions to individuals or groups when participants are all about the same age.

Variations

The themes used for the quizzes may be adapted in many different ways to create novelty, variety and fun. An example is a criss-cross quiz, using only a few of the themes.

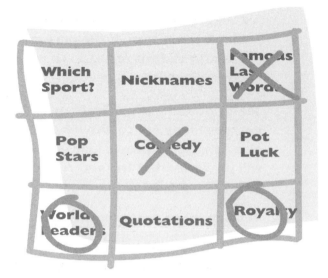

To play this game, draw on a board a large square with nine smaller squares inside, as shown above. Write the title of a quiz theme in each square. Divide participants into two teams, one to represent noughts and the other crosses. Toss a coin to decide which team answers first. That team then selects the subject on which they want to answer a question. If they get it right, their symbol is written in the appropriate square. The other team then chooses a subject on which to answer a question. The game continues in this fashion until one team has a row of noughts or crosses. That team can then be declared the winner. Using the quizzes in this way can add enormously to the novelty and fun.

This book is intended to stimulate you into making more diverse use of quizzes and creating some of your own. You can show photographs, slides or newspaper cuttings of famous people. Pictures of famous buildings or landmarks, or headlines about important events can be collected. Brief excerpts from music cassettes can be used, or snatches from tunes played on a musical instrument. It is an easy matter to compile quizzes about pop groups, radio or television series, local personalities, places, and so on. The scope is enormous. When compiling quizzes, bear in mind that questions need to be based on everyday subjects and general knowledge that most people could reasonably be expected to answer.

Quizzes are a good way of keeping people informed about the world. They encourage them to interact, share knowledge, use memory skills, reminisce or simply have fun. As such they provide an ideal tool for occupational therapists, nurses, teachers, social workers, care assistants or anybody organizing an activities programme. It is hoped that this book will inspire you.

Ted Payne was an area manager with the Royal Mail and wrote quizzes for brewery and newspaper leagues as well as charity competitions. Ted enjoyed playing for local pub teams, browsing in bookshops, following horse racing and formula one motor racing. When he wasn't researching questions, he and his wife Maureen served as local councillors. Sadly, Ted passed away and is survived by his wife and two sons.

Robin Dynes is a trained counsellor who has worked in the probation service, a number of psychiatric hospitals and private practice. He currently manages a mental health day centre that provides a variety of therapeutic and life-skill groups, including social and creative activities as well as individual counselling. He has many years of experience in working with groups and with individuals.

In addition to editing *Quiz Book for Groups: Famous People*, Robin is the author of *Creative Games in Groupwork* (1988), *Creative Writing in Groupwork* (1990), *The Reminiscence Puzzle Book* (1995), *The Non-Competitive Activity Book* (2000) and *Anxiety Management: A Practical Approach* (2001), all published by Speechmark Publishing.

Section 1

ANSWERS

Surnames Beginning with A & B

1 | **Larry Adler**

2 | **Louisa May Alcott**

3 | **Jane Austen**

4 | **Clement Attlee**

5 | **Fred Astaire**

6 | **Idi Amin**

7 | **Laura Ashley**

8 | **Neil Armstrong**

9 | **André Ampère**

10 | **Muhammad Ali**

QUESTIONS

Surnames Beginning with A & B

From the clues given, complete the names of the following people:

1   An American musician who was a virtuoso performer on the harmonica.

Larry **A**

2   The American author of the children's classic, *Little Women*.

Louisa May **A**

3   An English novelist, famous for such works as *Pride and Prejudice* and *Persuasion*.

Jane **A**

4   He was British Labour prime minister from 1945 to 1951.

Clement **A**

5   An American dancer, singer and actor who was famous as the partner of Ginger Rogers.

Fred **A**

6   The Ugandan president and dictator from 1971 until his flight from his country in 1979 following a Tanzania-backed rebellion.

Idi **A**

7   A Welsh designer who established — and gave her name to — a neo-Victorian style of clothing and furnishings.

Laura **A**

8   The first person to set foot on the moon.

Neil **A**

9   The French physicist and mathematician who made many discoveries in the field of electromagnetism and has a unit of electricity named after him.

André **A**

10   The first boxer to hold the world heavyweight title three times.

Muhammad **A**

11	**Anne Boleyn**
12	**William Booth**
13	**Napoleon Bonaparte**
14	**Boris Becker**
15	**Clyde Barrow**
16	**Charlotte Brontë**
17	**Yul Brynner**
18	**George Bush**
19	**Richard Burton**
20	**Jack Brabham**

QUESTIONS

11 The second wife of King Henry VIII.

> Anne B

12 The founder of the Salvation Army.

> William B

13 The emperor of France who was defeated at Waterloo.

> Napoleon B

14 The German tennis player who won his first Wimbledon title in 1985.

> Boris B

15 The American gangster whose partner was Bonnie Parker.

> Clyde B

16 She wrote the novels *Jane Eyre* and *Shirley*.

> Charlotte B

17 An American actor whose best films included *The Magnificent Seven* and *The King and I*.

> Yul B

18 The American president before Bill Clinton.

> George B

19 A Welsh film actor who was married to Elizabeth Taylor.

> Richard B

20 The Australian world champion Formula One driver in 1959, 1960 and 1966.

> Jack B

Which Sport?

1 **Motor racing**

2 **Boxing**

3 **Swimming**

4 **Tennis**

5 **Equestrianism**

6 **Baseball**

7 **Horse racing**

8 **Cricket**

9 **Soccer**

10 **Cycling**

QUESTIONS

Which Sport?

 In which sport were or are the following personalities involved?

1 Nelson Piquet

sailing	☐
motor racing	☐
soccer	☐

2 George Foreman

cricket	☐
baseball	☐
boxing	☐

3 Mark Spitz

swimming	☐
bowls	☐
cricket	☐

4 Billie Jean King

swimming	☐
tennis	☐
gymnastics	☐

5 Harvey Smith

shooting	☐
baseball	☐
equestrianism	☐

6 Joe Di Maggio

baseball	☐
boxing	☐
basketball	☐

7 Willie Shoemaker

horse racing	☐
motor cycling	☐
cricket	☐

8 Dennis Lillee

cricket	☐
horseracing	☐
swimming	☐

9 George Best

swimming	☐
soccer	☐
boxing	☐

10 Greg Lemond

wrestling	☐
squash	☐
cycling	☐

11 Boxing

12 Marathon

13 Running

14 Golf

15 Swimming

16 Tennis

17 Horse racing

18 Tennis

19 Soccer

20 Running

QUESTIONS

11 Rocky Marciano

boxing	☐
fencing	☐
wrestling	☐

12 Lisa Martin

discus	☐
marathon	☐
long jump	☐

13 Steve Ovett

basketball	☐
soccer	☐
running	☐

14 Gary Player

tennis	☐
rugby	☐
golf	☐

15 Dawn Fraser

eventing	☐
hurdling	☐
swimming	☐

16 Steffi Graf

tennis	☐
bowls	☐
archery	☐

17 Lester Piggott

golf	☐
bowls	☐
horse racing	☐

18 Björn Borg

tennis	☐
motor cycling	☐
ice hockey	☐

19 Bobby Charlton

cricket	☐
soccer	☐
motor racing	☐

20 Sebastian Coe

bowls	☐
fencing	☐
running	☐

ANSWERS

Pot Luck

1 | **Charles Dickens**

2 | **William Shakespeare**

3 | **Pat Garrett**

4 | **Ronald Reagan**

5 | **Alan Ladd**

6 | **George Gershwin**

7 | **Richard I**

8 | **Lou Costello**

9 | **Goolagong**

10 | **Jayne Torvill**

QUESTIONS

Pot Luck

Fill in the answers to the following general knowledge questions about famous people:

1 Who wrote *David Copperfield*?

2 Ann Hathaway was married to which famous playwright?

3 Who shot Billy the Kid?

4 Who was president of the USA in 1985?

5 Which actor starred as Shane in the film of the same name?

6 Who composed the music for *Porgy and Bess*?

7 Which English king was nicknamed 'The Lionheart'?

8 Who was Budd Abbott's stage and film partner?

9 What was the maiden name of the tennis player, Evonne Cawley?

10 Who skated to Olympic gold with Christopher Dean?

ANSWERS

11 Bruce Springsteen

12 Sir Edmund Hillary

13 John Travolta

14 Robert Louis Stevenson

15 Cliff Richard

16 Brazilian

17 Rossini

18 Tupelo

19 Greta Garbo

20 Paddington Bear

11   **Which American rock singer is nicknamed 'The Boss'?**

12   **Sherpa Tenzing and which other climber were the first to reach the summit of Everest in 1953?**

13   **Who starred with Olivia Newton-John in the film _Grease_?**

14   **Which famous author is buried on Samoa?**

15   **Which pop star had a hit with the song 'Congratulations'?**

16   **What nationality is the motor racing driver, Emerson Fittipaldi?**

17   **Who wrote the music for the opera, _The Barber of Seville_?**

18   **In which Mississippi town was Elvis Presley born?**

19   **Who said 'I want to be alone'?**

20   **Michael Bond created which bear with the same name as a London railway station?**

Real Names

1 | **Julie Andrews**

2 | **Charles Bronson**

3 | **David Bowie**

4 | **Woody Allen**

5 | **Michael Caine**

6 | **Richard Burton**

7 | **Cher**

8 | **Tony Curtis**

9 | **Elvis Costello**

10 | **Bob Dylan**

QUESTIONS

Real Names

 Choose from the three celebrities listed the one whose real name is given:

1 Julia Wells

Julie Andrews	☐
Juliet Mills	☐
Goldie Hawn	☐

2 Charles Buchinski

Charlton Heston	☐
Charles Bronson	☐
Charlie Sheen	☐

3 David Jones

Bruce Springsteen	☐
David Bowie	☐
Prince	☐

4 Allen Konigsberg

Woody Allen	☐
Steve Martin	☐
Mel Brooks	☐

5 Maurice Micklewhite

Mel Smith	☐
Sean Connery	☐
Michael Caine	☐

6 Richard Jenkins

James Cagney	☐
Steve McQueen	☐
Richard Burton	☐

7 Cherilyn La Pierre

Cher	☐
Madonna	☐
Goldie Hawn	☐

8 Bernard Schwartz

Steve Martin	☐
Tony Curtis	☐
Frank Sinatra	☐

9 Declan McManus

Elvis Costello	☐
Boy George	☐
Tom Jones	☐

10 Robert Allen Zimmermann

Bob Newhart	☐
Robert Redford	☐
Bob Dylan	☐

ANSWERS

11	Cliff Richard

12	Kirk Douglas

13	Neil Diamond

14	Elton John

15	Perry Como

16	Stan Laurel

17	Judy Garland

18	Stewart Granger

19	Boy George

20	Rita Hayworth

11 Harold Webb

Cliff Richard	☐
Mick Jagger	☐
Rod Stewart	☐

12 Issur Danielovich

Kirk Douglas	☐
Howard Keel	☐
Burt Lancaster	☐

13 Noah Kaminsky

Barry Manilow	☐
Neil Diamond	☐
Garth Brooks	☐

14 Reginald Dwight

Jasper Carrot	☐
Bob Hoskins	☐
Elton John	☐

15 Nick Perido

Dean Martin	☐
Frank Sinatra	☐
Perry Como	☐

16 Arthur Stanley Jefferson

Stan Laurel	☐
Buster Keaton	☐
Oliver Hardy	☐

17 Frances Gumm

Judy Garland	☐
Mae West	☐
Jean Harlow	☐

18 James Stewart

James Garner	☐
Stewart Granger	☐
Humphrey Bogart	☐

19 George O'Dowd

Johnny Cash	☐
Boy George	☐
Bill Haley	☐

20 Marguerita Cansino

Joan Crawford	☐
Greta Garbo	☐
Rita Hayworth	☐

ANSWERS

Westerns

1 | Kevin Costner

2 | Clint Eastwood

3 | Jane Russell

4 | John Wayne

5 | 'Do Not Forsake Me, O'My Darlin'

6 | Roy Rogers

7 | Gene Autry

8 | The Sundance Kid

9 | Lee Marvin

10 | A Japanese farmer to give him a medal won by his dead son.

Westerns

Fill in the answers to the following general knowledge questions:

1 Who both directed and starred in the film *Dances With Wolves*?

2 Who played the stranger who rides into town and proceeds to paint all the buildings red in *High Plains Drifter*?

3 Who was the leading lady in the film *The Outlaw*?

4 Which actor, who starred in many westerns, was known as 'Duke'?

5 Which song did Tex Ritter sing that provided the theme tune for *High Noon*?

6 Which western star rode a horse called 'Trigger'?

7 Who was known as the singing cowboy?

8 Who was Butch Cassidy's partner?

9 Who played the drunken has-been gunfighter in the comedy western *Cat Ballou*?

10 Who was Spencer Tracy looking for when he arrived in Black Rock in the film *Bad Day at Black Rock*?

ANSWERS

11 His niece who had been kidnapped by the commanches.

12 Tonto

13 Audie Murphy

14 Dean Martin

15 James Garner

16 William Holden

17 Calamity Jane

18 Betty Hutton

19 Yul Brynner

20 Wyatt Earp

QUESTIONS

11 Who was John Wayne looking for in the film *The Searchers*?

12 Who was the Lone Ranger's partner?

13 Who was America's most decorated soldier of the Second World War who played the roles of Jessie James and Billy the Kid?

14 Which singing star played the drunken deputy sheriff 'Dude' in the film *Rio Bravo*?

15 Who played Bret Maverick in the TV series *Maverick*?

16 Who played the ruthless outlaw leader in *The Wild Bunch*?

17 In which film did Doris Day sing 'Oh, the Deadwood Stage is a headin' on over the hills'?

18 Who played the title role in the film *Annie Get Your Gun*?

19 Who played the leader of the gang of gunfighters defending a poor Mexican farming village against a vicious bandit gang?

20 Who was the lawman who faced the Clantons in *Gunfight at the OK Corral*?

Section 2

ANSWERS

Surnames Beginning with C & D

1 **Julius Caesar**

2 **Fidel Castro**

3 **William Caxton**

4 **Neville Chamberlain**

5 **Jacques Cousteau**

6 **Bing Crosby**

7 **Peter Cushing**

8 **Charles Cruft**

9 **Captain James Cook**

10 **John Constable**

Surnames Beginning with C & D

From the clues given, complete the names of the following people:

1 The Roman emperor assassinated on the 'Ides of March'.

Julius C

2 The ruler of Cuba from 1959.

Fidel C

3 Recognized as the first English printer.

William C

4 The British prime minister at the outbreak of the Second World War.

Neville C

5 The French underwater explorer who pioneered techniques in underwater photography.

Jacques C

6 An American singer and actor, famous for the song 'White Christmas'.

Bing C

7 A British actor, well known for his roles in horror films.

Peter C

8 The founder of a famous British dog show.

Charles C

9 An English explorer who made voyages of discovery to Australia and New Zealand.

Captain James C

10 An English artist, one of whose well known works is *The Haywain*.

John C

11 | Salvador Dali

12 | Frederick Delius

13 | John Dillinger

14 | 'Fats' Domino

15 | Lorna Doone

16 | John Boyd Dunlop

17 | Benjamin Disraeli

18 | Marlene Dietrich

19 | Leonardo Da Vinci

20 | Charles Darwin

11 An eccentric surrealist painter from Spain.

Salvador **D**

12 An English composer whose works included 'Sea Drift' and 'A Song Of Summer'.

Frederick **D**

13 An American gangster who was given the title of 'Public Enemy No I'.

John **D**

14 An American rock and roll pianist whose hits include 'Blueberry Hill' and 'Ain't That a Shame'.

'Fats' **D**

15 The heroine of RD Blackmore's novel of the same name.

Lorna **D**

16 The Scottish inventor who founded the rubber company which bears his name.

John Boyd **D**

17 The 19th-century British prime minister who became the Earl of Beaconsfield.

Benjamin **D**

18 A German film actress whose films included *Destry Rides Again* and *The Blue Angel*.

Marlene **D**

19 The famous Italian renaissance artist who painted the *Mona Lisa*.

Leonardo **D**

20 The English scientist who developed the modern theory of evolution.

Charles **D**

ANSWERS

World Leaders

1 | France

2 | Russia

3 | Ireland

4 | Iraq

5 | USA

6 | West Germany

7 | Great Britain

8 | Egypt

9 | Canada

10 | Ethiopia

QUESTIONS

World Leaders

 The person named is associated with which country?

1 Charles de Gaulle

Italy	☐
Spain	☐
France	☐

2 Alexei Kosygin

Russia	☐
Hungary	☐
Poland	☐

3 Eamon de Valera

Portugal	☐
Brazil	☐
Ireland	☐

4 Saddam Hussein

Iran	☐
Iraq	☐
Jordan	☐

5 Herbert Hoover

Canada	☐
Australia	☐
USA	☐

6 Willy Brandt

West Germany	☐
Sweden	☐
Denmark	☐

7 Winston Churchill

Canada	☐
New Zealand	☐
Great Britain	☐

8 Gamal Nasser

Egypt	☐
Turkey	☐
Cyprus	☐

9 Pierre Trudeau

Canada	☐
Belgium	☐
Switzerland	☐

10 Haile Selassie

Ethiopia	☐
Angola	☐
Nigeria	☐

11 | Australia

12 | Rhodesia

13 | Egypt

14 | Denmark

15 | Spain

16 | USA

17 | Britain

18 | Jordan

19 | New Zealand

20 | Poland

QUESTIONS

11 Malcolm Fraser

New Zealand	☐
South Africa	☐
Australia	☐

12 Ian Smith

Kenya	☐
Rhodesia	☐
Uganda	☐

13 King Farouk

Egypt	☐
Libya	☐
Saudi Arabia	☐

14 Queen Margrethe II

Italy	☐
Denmark	☐
Austria	☐

15 Francisco Franco

Greece	☐
Spain	☐
Italy	☐

16 Abraham Lincoln

USA	☐
Ireland	☐
Israel	☐

17 Harold Wilson

Australia	☐
Canada	☐
Britain	☐

18 King Hussein

Saudi Arabia	☐
Syria	☐
Jordan	☐

19 Jim Bolger

New Zealand	☐
Ireland	☐
Jamaica	☐

20 Lech Walesa

Romania	☐
Bulgaria	☐
Poland	☐

ANSWERS

Pot Luck

1 **Paul McCartney**

2 **Skytrain**

3 *True Grit*

4 **Tchaikovsky**

5 **Little Big Horn**

6 **Vincent Van Gogh**

7 **Corsica**

8 *Charlie's Angels*

9 **Noel Coward**

10 **Sherwood Forest**

Pot Luck

Fill in the answers to the following general knowledge questions about famous people:

1 Which member of the Beatles formed the group 'Wings'?

2 What name did Freddie Laker give to his cut-price air service launched in 1977?

3 John Wayne was awarded an Oscar for which film?

4 Who composed *Swan Lake*?

5 General George Armstrong Custer died fighting which battle?

6 Which Dutch artist cut off his ear?

7 Napoleon Bonaparte was born on which island?

8 The actresses Jaclyn Smith and Kate Jackson played two of three title roles in which TV series?

9 Who said: 'Don't put your daughter on the stage, Mrs Worthington'?

10 Robin Hood hid in which forest?

ANSWERS

11 Alan Shepard

12 Harpo

13 Beatrix Potter

14 Cuba

15 The C5 pedal-powered tricycle

16 Sandie Shaw

17 Carmel

18 Thomas Hardy

19 Erwin Rommel

20 Dame Nellie Melba (Peach Melba)

QUESTIONS

11   Who was the first American in space?

12   Adolph Marx was the real name of which of the Marx brothers?

13   Who created Jemima Puddle-duck and Mrs Tittlemouse?

14   Fidel Castro has ruled which country for more than 30 years?

15   Which mode of transport was launched in January 1985 by Clive Sinclair?

16   Which barefoot pop star won the 1967 *Eurovision Song Contest* with the song 'Puppet On A String'?

17   Clint Eastwood became mayor of which town in 1986?

18   Who wrote *Tess of the D'Urbervilles*?

19   Which German field marshal commanded the Afrika Korps in the Second World War?

20   Which opera singer has an ice-cream dessert named after her?

ANSWERS

Oscar-Winning Actresses

1 **Glenda Jackson**

2 **Jane Fonda**

3 **Liza Minnelli**

4 **Katharine Hepburn**

5 **Sally Field**

6 **Julie Christie**

7 **Audrey Hepburn**

8 **Jessica Tandy**

9 **Elizabeth Taylor**

10 **Maggie Smith**

Oscar-Winning Actresses

 From the three given actresses, choose which one was awarded an Oscar for the film named:

1 Women in Love

Glenda Jackson	☐
Susannah York	☐
Glenn Close	☐

2 Klute

Sophia Loren	☐
Goldie Hawn	☐
Jane Fonda	☐

3 Cabaret

Mia Farrow	☐
Jodie Foster	☐
Liza Minnelli	☐

4 Guess Who's Coming To Dinner

Bette Davis	☐
Katharine Hepburn	☐
Ingrid Bergman	☐

5 Norma Rae

Meryl Streep	☐
Diane Keaton	☐
Sally Field	☐

6 Darling

Jane Fonda	☐
Elizabeth Taylor	☐
Julie Christie	☐

7 Roman Holiday

Deborah Kerr	☐
Audrey Hepburn	☐
Doris Day	☐

8 Driving Miss Daisy

Jessica Tandy	☐
Whoopi Goldberg	☐
Shirley Maclaine	☐

9 Butterfield 8

Susan Hayward	☐
Elizabeth Taylor	☐
Carroll Baker	☐

10 The Prime of Miss Jean Brodie

Glenda Jackson	☐
Rita Hayworth	☐
Maggie Smith	☐

ANSWERS

11 Anne Bancroft

12 Elizabeth Taylor

13 Diane Keaton

14 Meryl Streep

15 Olivia De Havilland

16 Greer Garson

17 Shirley Maclaine

18 Sissy Spacek

19 Katharine Hepburn

20 Julie Andrews

QUESTIONS

11 *The Miracle Worker*

Patricia Neal	☐
Vivien Leigh	☐
Anne Bancroft	☐

12 *Who's Afraid of Virginia Woolf?*

Jane Russell	☐
Bette Davis	☐
Elizabeth Taylor	☐

13 *Annie Hall*

Sally Field	☐
Diane Keaton	☐
Mitzi Gaynor	☐

14 *Sophie's Choice*

Meryl Streep	☐
Faye Dunaway	☐
Geraldine Page	☐

15 *The Heiress*

Vivien Leigh	☐
Olivia De Havilland	☐
Jane Wayman	☐

16 *Mrs Miniver*

Greer Garson	☐
Joan Crawford	☐
Bette Davis	☐

17 *Terms of Endearment*

Debbie Reynolds	☐
Shirley Maclaine	☐
Liza Minnelli	☐

18 *The Coal Miner's Daughter*

Sissy Spacek	☐
Kathy Bates	☐
Meg Ryan	☐

19 *On Golden Pond*

Elizabeth Taylor	☐
Katharine Hepburn	☐
Glenda Jackson	☐

20 *Mary Poppins*

Julie Andrews	☐
Julie Christie	☐
Jane Fonda	☐

ANSWERS

People from the Bible

1   **Delilah**

2   **Barabbas**

3   **Saul**

4   **Moses**

5   **Goliath**

6   **Luke**

7   **Joseph**

8   **Judas Iscariot**

9   **John the Baptist**

10   **John**

QUESTIONS

People from the Bible

Fill in the answers to the following general knowledge questions about biblical people:

1 Which woman seduced and betrayed Samson?

2 Which robber was freed instead of Jesus?

3 Who was the first king of Israel?

4 Who led the children of Israel out of Egypt?

5 What was the name of the giant killed by David?

6 Which of the disciples was a physician?

7 Who was the favourite son of Jacob and Rachel?

8 Who was paid 30 pieces of silver?

9 Who baptised Jesus?

10 Who was the youngest of the disciples?

11 | **Andrew**

12 | **Pontius Pilate**

13 | **Jeremiah**

14 | **Jonah**

15 | **Cain**

16 | **Moses**

17 | **Jesus**

18 | **Solomon**

19 | **Matthew**

20 | **Noah**

QUESTIONS

11 Which disciple was the brother of Peter?

12 Who said: 'I find no fault in this man'?

13 Which prophet foretold the destruction of Jerusalem?

14 Who was swallowed by a great fish?

15 Who was the first son of Adam and Eve?

16 Who received the ten commandments from God?

17 Who fasted for 40 days and nights in the wilderness?

18 Who was described as the wisest and wealthiest of the kings of Israel?

19 Which of the disciples was a tax collector?

20 Who did God instruct to build an ark?

Section3

Surnames Beginning with E & F

1 Edward Elgar

2 Ralph Waldo Emerson

3 Chris Evert

4 Brian Epstein

5 George Eliot

6 Dame Edith Evans

7 Dwight Eisenhower

8 Albert Einstein

9 Gareth Edwards

10 Amelia Earhart

Surnames Beginning with E & F

From the clues given, complete the names of the following people:

1 A British composer whose major works included *The Dream of Gerontius* and *Pomp and Circumstance.*

> Edward E

2 A famous American poet who was born in Boston.

> Ralph Waldo E

3 An American tennis player who became the first female player to win one million dollars in prize money.

> Chris E

4 The manager of the Beatles.

> Brian E

5 The English novelist who wrote *Middlemarch* and *The Mill on the Floss.*

> George E

6 A British actress who was renowned for her role as Lady Bracknell in *The Importance of Being Ernest.*

> Dame Edith E

7 The President of the USA from 1953 to 1961.

> Dwight E

8 The German-born scientist who formulated the theory of relativity.

> Albert E

9 A top Welsh rugby player who was only 20 years old when he was appointed captain of his country.

> Gareth E

10 The first woman to fly the Atlantic solo.

> Amelia E

ANSWERS

11 Peter Carl Fabergé

12 Guy Fawkes

13 Gustave Flaubert

14 William George Fargo

15 Henry Fielding

16 Errol Flynn

17 Margot Fonteyn

18 Henry Ford

19 Sigmund Freud

20 F Scott Fitzgerald

11 A Russian goldsmith and jeweller, who was famous for his jewelled Easter eggs.

Peter Carl **F**

12 An English conspirator in the Gunpowder Plot to blow up King James I and his parliament.

Guy **F**

13 The French novelist who wrote *Madame Bovary*.

Gustave **F**

14 An American transport pioneer who established a famous freight company.

William George **F**

15 The author of *Tom Jones*.

Henry **F**

16 An Australian film star, famous for action roles in such films as *Captain Blood* and *The Sea Hawk*.

Errol **F**

17 An English ballet dancer who was renowned for her perfect physique and interpretative powers.

Margot **F**

18 Founder of a major automobile company.

Henry **F**

19 The Austrian psychiatrist who pioneered the study of the unconscious mind.

Sigmund **F**

20 An American writer whose novels included *This Side of Paradise* and *The Great Gatsby*.

F Scott **F**

People and Places

1 | Rochdale

2 | Broadlands

3 | Arabia

4 | Australia

5 | Liverpool

6 | Russia

7 | Chartwell

8 | Coniston Water

9 | Dove Cottage

10 | Ireland

QUESTIONS

People and Places

From the alternatives given, choose the place with which the famous person has been associated:

1 Gracie Fields

Rochdale	☐
Derby	☐
Lancaster	☐

2 Earl Mountbatten of Burma

York House	☐
Broadlands	☐
Sandringham	☐

3 TE Lawrence

Iran	☐
Arabia	☐
Iraq	☐

4 Donald Bradman

Australia	☐
India	☐
South Africa	☐

5 Cilla Black

Preston	☐
Manchester	☐
Liverpool	☐

6 Peter the Great

Russia	☐
Germany	☐
Greece	☐

7 Winston Churchill

Chartwell	☐
Lambeth Palace	☐
Norfolk House	☐

8 Donald Campbell

Loch Ness	☐
Coniston Water	☐
Loch Lomond	☐

9 William Wordsworth

Dove Cottage	☐
Eastwood	☐
Blenheim Palace	☐

10 Mary Peters

Canada	☐
Wales	☐
Ireland	☐

11   **Osborne House**

12   **Wales**

13   **The Scilly Isles**

14   **Canada**

15   **Howarth Parsonage**

16   **Tintagel**

17   **South Africa**

18   **Antarctic**

19   **Dorset**

20   **Poland**

11 Queen Victoria

Osborne House ☐

Marlborough House ☐

Barnwell Manor ☐

12 Tom Jones

Wales ☐

Scotland ☐

Ireland ☐

13 Harold Wilson

The Scilly Isles ☐

Isle of Man ☐

The Orkney Islands ☐

14 Isadora Duncan

Canada ☐

America ☐

Australia ☐

15 The Brontë Sisters

Haworth Parsonage ☐

Max Gate ☐

Menabilly ☐

16 King Arthur

Perranporth ☐

Tintagel ☐

Bude ☐

17 Zola Budd

Kenya ☐

South Africa ☐

Australia ☐

18 Captain Robert Scott

Antarctic ☐

Arctic ☐

Mount Everest ☐

19 Thomas Hardy

Somerset ☐

Dorset ☐

Devon ☐

20 Lech Walesa

Poland ☐

Russia ☐

Yugoslavia ☐

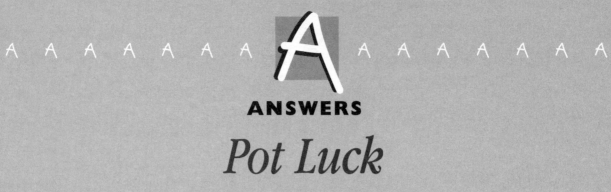

ANSWERS

Pot Luck

1 **John Major**

2 **Yuri Gagarin**

3 **Judy Garland**

4 **The Atlantic**

5 **Philip Marlowe**

6 **John Lennon**

7 **Burt Lancaster**

8 **Sting**

9 **George Harrison**

10 **Man Friday**

Pot Luck

Fill in the answers to the following general knowledge questions about famous people:

1 Who replaced Margaret Thatcher as British prime minister?

2 Which Russian was the first person in space?

3 Who was Liza Minnelli's famous mother?

4 Charles Lindbergh made the first non-stop flight across which ocean in 1927?

5 Raymond Chandler created which famous private detective?

6 Which famous singer and songwriter was married to Yoko Ono?

7 Which actor played the title role in the film *The Birdman of Alcatraz*?

8 Gordon Sumner is the real name of which singer with a single name?

9 Who was the youngest of the Beatles?

10 What was the name of Robinson Crusoe's companion?

11 | Hopalong Cassidy

12 | Holland

13 | The Archbishop of Canterbury

14 | President John F Kennedy

15 | King John

16 | Horse racing

17 | Cricket

18 | Fashion

19 | James Bond

20 | HG Wells

11 William Boyd played which famous TV and film cowboy?

12 Johan Cruyff played soccer for which country?

13 Lambeth Palace is the home of which religious leader?

14 Which American president said, 'Ich bin ein Berliner'?

15 Which English king signed the Magna Carta?

16 The Aga Khan is famous for his sponsorship of which sport?

17 Douglas Jardine led the England team responsible for the bodyline disagreement in which sport in the 1930s?

18 Yves St Laurent achieved fame in which field?

19 Which film hero preferred his Martinis shaken and not stirred?

20 Who wrote *The Time Machine*?

ANSWERS

Quotations

1 | Marie Antoinette

2 | Liberace

3 | Henry Ford

4 | George Orwell

5 | Elizabeth I

6 | Muhammad Ali

7 | Winston Churchill

8 | John F Kennedy

9 | Mark Twain

10 | JK Galbraith

QUESTIONS

Quotations

 From the three alternatives given, choose who was responsible for the quotation:

1 "Let them eat cake."

Mrs Beeton ☐

Marie Antoinette ☐

Margaret Thatcher ☐

2 "I cried all the way to the bank."

Liberace ☐

Mae West ☐

Winston Churchill ☐

3 "History is bunk."

Henry Ford ☐

Jean Paul Getty ☐

Theodore Roosevelt ☐

4 "All animals are equal, but some are more equal than others."

WC Fields ☐

George Orwell ☐

Benito Mussolini ☐

5 "I know I have the body of a weak and feeble woman, but I have the heart and stomach of a king."

Mary Queen of Scots ☐

Cleopatra ☐

Elizabeth I ☐

6 "I am the greatest."

Muhammad Ali ☐

Nigel Mansell ☐

Donald Bradman ☐

7 "I have nothing to offer but blood, toil, tears and sweat."

Margaret Thatcher ☐

David Lloyd George ☐

Winston Churchill ☐

8 "Ask not what your country can do for you, but what you can do for your country."

John F Kennedy ☐

Ronald Reagan ☐

Dwight Eisenhower ☐

9 "Reports of my death have been greatly exaggerated."

Oscar Wilde ☐

Mark Twain ☐

Vincent Van Gogh ☐

10 "There is no such thing as a free lunch."

PT Barnum ☐

JK Galbraith ☐

TS Eliot ☐

11 Samuel Johnson

12 Queen Victoria

13 Tennyson

14 General MacArthur

15 Milton

16 Henry II

17 McEnroe

18 Shaw

19 Duke of Wellington

20 Abraham Lincoln

QUESTIONS

11 "When a man knows he is to be hanged in a fortnight it concentrates his mind wonderfully."

Samuel Johnson ☐
Samuel Pepys ☐
Samuel Colt ☐

12 "We are not amused."

Queen Victoria ☐
Lady Macbeth ☐
Nancy Reagan ☐

13 "Theirs not to reason why, theirs but to do and die."

Wordsworth ☐
Shakespeare ☐
Tennyson ☐

14 "Old soldiers never die, they simply fade away."

Napoleon Bonaparte ☐
Dwight Eisenhower ☐
General MacArthur ☐

15 "They also serve who only stand and wait."

Keats ☐
Milton ☐
Wordsworth ☐

16 "Will no one rid me of this turbulent priest?"

William I ☐
George III ☐
Henry II ☐

17 "You cannot be serious!"

Becker ☐
McEnroe ☐
Borg ☐

18 "Youth is wasted on the young."

Shaw ☐
Kipling ☐
Keats ☐

19 "Publish and be damned!"

Duke of York ☐
Duke of Wellington ☐
Duke of Cornwall ☐

20 "Government of the people, by the people, for the people."

John F Kennedy ☐
Abraham Lincoln ☐
Franklin Roosevelt ☐

ANSWERS
Pop Stars

1   **Connie Francis**

2   **The Beatles**

3   **Buddy Holly**

4   **Gracie Fields**

5   **Vera Lynn**

6   **Bob Geldof**

7   **Perry Como**

8   **The Everly Brothers**

9   **Bill Haley**

10   **Elvis Presley**

Pop Stars

 Fill in the answers to the following general knowledge questions about famous people:

1 Who was the American singing star of the 1950s and 1960s whose hits included 'Lipstick On Your Collar' and 'Robot Man'?

2 'Let It Be' was the last song recorded by which group?

3 Which legendary singer who died in an aircrash made the hit recordings 'Peggy Sue' and 'That'll Be the Day'?

4 Who sang about the 'Biggest Aspidistra in the World'?

5 Which singer had wartime hits with 'We'll Meet Again' and 'The White Cliffs of Dover'?

6 Which Irish pop star promoted the charity pop concert called 'Live Aid'?

7 Which American star had the hits 'Magic Moments', 'Catch A Falling Star' and 'Delaware'?

8 'Wake Up Little Susie' and 'Bye Bye Love' were hits from which pop duo?

9 Which rock star had a hit with 'Rock Around the Clock'?

10 Who lived in a mansion called 'Graceland' in Memphis?

ANSWERS

11 The Sex Pistols

12 Diana Ross

13 Roy Orbison

14 Shirley Bassey

15 Gary Glitter

16 Jazz

17 Michael Jackson

18 Sandie Shaw

19 Tom Jones

20 Louis Armstrong

11 Johnny Rotten and Sid Vicious belonged to which group?

12 Who was the leader of the 1960s all-girl pop group, The Supremes?

13 Which male singer had hits with 'Only The Lonely', 'Running Scared' and 'Pretty Woman'?

14 Who sang the title songs for the James Bond films, *Goldfinger* and *Moonraker*?

15 Who sang 'I'm the Leader of the Gang'?

16 What kind of music did Ella Fitzgerald become famous for singing?

17 Which American singer had a hit with his album entitled 'Thriller'?

18 Who had the hits 'Always There to Remind Me', 'Monsieur Dupont' and 'Puppet on a String'?

19 Which pop star had the hit 'It's Not Unusual'?

20 Which jazz trumpeter and singer had hits with 'Hello Dolly' and 'What a Wonderful World'?

Section 4

Surnames Beginning with G & H

1 | **Clark Gable**

2 | **Thomas Gainsborough**

3 | **Mahatma Gandhi**

4 | **Greta Garbo**

5 | **George Gershwin**

6 | **WS Gilbert**

7 | **Edvard Grieg**

8 | **Billy Graham**

9 | **Paul Gauguin**

10 | **Sir Alec Guinness**

Surnames Beginning with G & H

From the clues given, complete the names of the following people:

1 An American actor, nicknamed 'The King of Hollywood', fondly remembered for his portrayal of Rhett Butler in *Gone with the Wind*.

Clark G

2 An English landscape and portrait artist who was born in Sudbury, Suffolk in 1727.

Thomas G

3 The Indian nationalist who led his country to independence.

Mahatma G

4 A legendary Swedish film actress who eventually shunned all publicity.

Greta G

5 An American composer who wrote many popular songs in partnership with his brother Ira.

George G

6 A British dramatist who worked with Arthur Sullivan to produce a famous series of light operas.

WS G

7 A Norwegian composer whose best known work is *Peer Gynt*.

Edvard G

8 A famous American evangelist whose revivalist meetings draw huge crowds around the world.

Billy G

9 A French post-impressionist artist who left Europe to paint in Tahiti.

Paul G

10 An English actor whose many films include *Bridge on the River Kwai* and *Kind Hearts and Coronets*.

Sir Alec G

11 **Anne Hathaway**

12 **Jimi Hendrix**

13 **James Herriot**

14 **Charles Haughey**

15 **Alfred Hitchcock**

16 **Gustav Holst**

17 **Ernest Hemingway**

18 **William Hartnell**

19 **Edward Heath**

20 **Engelbert Humperdinck**

11 The wife of William Shakespeare.

Anne **H**

12 A legendary rock guitarist, singer and songwriter who became famous for his experimental technique.

Jimi **H**

13 The pen name of James Alfred Wight, the English vet who wrote a popular series of books made into TV series and films.

James **H**

14 He has been Irish prime minister three times from 1979.

Charles **H**

15 An English director of suspense films.

Alfred **H**

16 The composer of the suite *The Planets*.

Gustav **H**

17 The author of *A Farewell to Arms*.

Ernest **H**

18 The British actor who played the first Doctor Who.

William **H**

19 He was the British prime minister from 1970 to 1974.

Edward **H**

20 An English singer whose hits in the 1960s included 'Release Me' and 'The Last Waltz'.

Engelbert **H**

ANSWERS
Great Composers

1 Gilbert and Sullivan

2 Tchaikovsky

3 Ravel

4 Handel

5 Bizet

6 Tchaikosvky

7 Johann Strauss

8 Liszt

9 Holst

10 Offenbach

Great Composers

 Which of the composers given wrote the following works?

1 The Mikado

Gilbert and Sullivan	☐
Chopin	☐
Elgar	☐

2 Swan Lake

Gershwin	☐
Tchaikovsky	☐
Grieg	☐

3 'Bolero'

Verdi	☐
Dvorak	☐
Ravel	☐

4 The Messiah

Handel	☐
Mantovani	☐
Lloyd-Webber	☐

5 Carmen

Elgar	☐
Bizet	☐
Mozart	☐

6 Sleeping Beauty

Tchaikovsky	☐
Puccini	☐
Sibelius	☐

7 'The Blue Danube'

Wagner	☐
Johann Strauss	☐
Mozart	☐

8 'Hungarian Rhapsody'

Liszt	☐
Brahms	☐
Chopin	☐

9 The Planets

Rachmaninov	☐
Mozart	☐
Holst	☐

10 Orpheus in the Underworld

Richard Strauss	☐
Handel	☐
Offenbach	☐

11 Richard Strauss

12 Beethoven

13 Tchaikovsky

14 Schubert

15 Gilbert and Sullivan

16 Mozart

17 Wagner

18 Elgar

19 Verdi

20 Chopin

QUESTIONS

11 Tales from the Vienna Woods

Richard Strauss	☐
Puccini	☐
Grieg	☐

12 The Pastoral

Brahms	☐
Mozart	☐
Beethoven	☐

13 '1812 Overture'

Vivaldi	☐
Rossini	☐
Tchaikovsky	☐

14 The Unfinished Symphony

Schubert	☐
Mozart	☐
Wagner	☐

15 The Gondoliers

Gilbert and Sullivan	☐
Chopin	☐
Elgar	☐

16 Don Giovanni

Mozart	☐
Britten	☐
Mendelssohn	☐

17 Tristan und Isolde

Mozart	☐
Wagner	☐
Beethoven	☐

18 Pomp and Circumstance

Grieg	☐
Holst	☐
Elgar	☐

19 La Traviata

Brahms	☐
Verdi	☐
Liszt	☐

20 'Minute Waltz'

Johann Strauss	☐
Chopin	☐
Dvorak	☐

Pot Luck

1 Edwin 'Buzz' Aldrin

2 Al Capone

3 Conducting

4 Abraham Lincoln

5 Margaret Thatcher

6 The flute

7 Leonardo da Vinci

8 Wolfgang Amadeus Mozart

9 The piano

10 Dwight D Eisenhower

QUESTIONS

Pot Luck

Fill in the answers to the following general knowledge questions about famous people:

1   Who was the second person to set foot on the moon?

2   Which American gangster nicknamed 'Scarface' was imprisoned in 1931 on a charge of tax evasion?

3   For what was Sir John Barbirolli renowned?

4   Which American president was shot dead in a theatre in 1865?

5   Which former prime minister has twin children named Carol and Mark?

6   Which instrument does James Galway play?

7   Who painted the famous enigmatic portrait, the *Mona Lisa*?

8   Which great composer had the middle name Amadeus?

9   Which musical instrument is associated with Richard Clayderman?

10 Which American president was nicknamed 'Ike'?

ANSWERS

11 John McEnroe

12 Shirley Temple

13 Sir Walter Raleigh

14 Photography

15 Hairdressing

16 *Treasure Island*

17 Bizet

18 Social Democrat Party (SDP)

19 Sir Winston Churchill

20 Dance

11 Which tennis player was nicknamed 'superbrat'?

12 Which child star of the 1930s sang about the 'Good Ship Lollipop'?

13 Who was said to have put his cloak over a muddy patch so that Queen Elizabeth I could cross it with dry feet?

14 For what are Lord Snowdon and Patrick Lichfield famous?

15 What did Vidal Sassoon do to become famous?

16 In which book do Ben Gunn and Long John Silver appear?

17 Who composed the opera *Carmen*?

18 Which political party was founded by Roy Jenkins?

19 Which British prime minister won the Nobel Prize for Literature?

20 What did Wayne Sleep do to become famous?

Fictional Characters

1 | **Raymond Chandler**

2 | **Bram Stoker**

3 | **PG Wodehouse**

4 | **Ruth Rendell**

5 | **Agatha Christie**

6 | **Margaret Mitchell**

7 | **Charles Dickens**

8 | **Daphne Du Maurier**

9 | **John Buchan**

10 | **Mark Twain**

QUESTIONS

Fictional Characters

 From the authors named, choose the one who created the following fictional characters:

1 Philip Marlowe

Raymond Chandler	☐
Norman Mailer	☐
Arthur Hailey	☐

2 Dracula

Edgar Allan Poe	☐
Bram Stoker	☐
Stephen King	☐

3 Bertie Wooster

HE Bates	☐
PG Wodehouse	☐
Rudyard Kipling	☐

4 Chief Inspector Wexford

Len Deighton	☐
John Le Carré	☐
Ruth Rendell	☐

5 Miss Marple

Agatha Christie	☐
Paul Gallico	☐
PD James	☐

6 Scarlett O'Hara

Gladys Mitchell	☐
Harper Lee	☐
Margaret Mitchell	☐

7 Mr Micawber

John Galsworthy	☐
Thomas Hardy	☐
Charles Dickens	☐

8 Rebecca

Daphne Du Maurier	☐
John Masefield	☐
Barbara Cartland	☐

9 Richard Hannay

John Buchan	☐
Alistair MacLean	☐
Ellery Queen	☐

10 Tom Sawyer

Morris West	☐
HG Wells	☐
Mark Twain	☐

11 James Thurber

12 Georges Simenon

13 Ian Fleming

14 James Joyce

15 Joseph Heller

16 Erle Stanley Gardner

17 Nicholas Freeling

18 Daniel Defoe

19 AJ Cronin

20 GK Chesterton

11 Walter Mitty

Anthony Burgess	☐
James Thurber	☐
Kingsley Amis	☐

12 Inspector Maigret

Eric Ambler	☐
Erskine Childers	☐
Georges Simenon	☐

13 James Bond

Ian Fleming	☐
Ross McDonald	☐
Peter Cheyney	☐

14 Molly Bloom

Jane Austen	☐
James Joyce	☐
Dylan Thomas	☐

15 Yossarian

Joseph Heller	☐
Ken Follett	☐
John O'Hara	☐

16 Perry Mason

Winston Graham	☐
Ed McBain	☐
Erle Stanley Gardner	☐

17 Inspector Van der Valk

Dick Francis	☐
Nicholas Freeling	☐
Frederick Forsyth	☐

18 Robinson Crusoe

Alexandre Dumas	☐
William Golding	☐
Daniel Defoe	☐

19 Dr Finlay

Graham Greene	☐
Georgette Heyer	☐
AJ Cronin	☐

20 Father Brown

GK Chesterton	☐
Mary Renault	☐
Edgar Wallace	☐

ANSWERS

20th-Century Men

1 Antarctica

2 Terry Waite

3 Howard Hughes

4 Presenting the BBC News

5 Ernest Bevin

6 The violin

7 Liberal

8 Boris Becker

9 Jeffrey Archer

10 Archbishop Makarios III

20th-Century Men

Fill in the answers to the following general knowledge questions about famous people:

1 Sir Vivian Fuchs led an expedition across which continent in 1957-8?

2 Which special representative of the Archbishop of Canterbury became a hostage?

3 Which American film maker and tycoon hid himself away from the public eye for over 25 years?

4 What did Robert Dougall become well known for doing?

5 Which British politician instigated a scheme for sending boys down the mines during the Second World War?

6 Which instrument did Yehudi Menuhin become famous for playing?

7 Which political party in the United Kingdom did Lloyd George lead?

8 Which 17-year-old German defeated Kevin Curren in 1985 to become the youngest Wimbledon men's champion in history?

9 Which British MP resigned after a financial disgrace and then launched a new career as a novelist with *Not a Penny More, Not a Penny Less*?

10 Which archbishop was elected the first president of Cyprus in December 1959?

ANSWERS

11   Robin Knox-Johnston

12   Edgar Rice Burroughs

13   Republican

14   HRH Prince Philip

15   Jesse Owens

16   Robert Baden-Powell

17   TS Eliot

18   South Africa

19   Mao Tse-tung

20   United Nations

11   Who was the first person to sail alone non-stop around the world?

12   Who wrote stories about Tarzan?

13   With which political party would you associate Ronald Reagan?

14   Who said: 'Dentopedology is the science of opening your mouth and putting your foot in it. I've practised it for years'?

15   Which black American athlete won four gold medals in the 1936 Berlin Olympics?

16   Who founded the Boy Scouts?

17   Which poet wrote *Old Possum's Book of Practical Cats*, on which the musical *Cats* is based?

18   In which country is Nelson Mandela a political leader?

19   Which Chinese leader directed the famous 'Long March' and later became head of State in the new Chinese People's Republic?

20   Dag Hammarskjöld became secretary-general of which organization?

Section5

Surnames Beginning with J & K

1 **Lyndon B Johnson**

2 **Al Jolson**

3 **Carl Jung**

4 **James Joyce**

5 **Mick Jagger**

6 **Jack Johnson**

7 **Jesse James**

8 **Dr Samuel Johnson**

9 **Jerome K Jerome**

10 **Tom Jones**

Surnames Beginning with J & K

From the clues given, complete the names of the following people:

1 The 36th president of the USA

| Lyndon B **J** |

2 A Russian-born singer and entertainer who lived in the USA from childhood and starred in the first talking picture, *The Jazz Singer*.

| Al **J** |

3 A Swiss psychiatrist born in Kesswill who developed the school of 'analytic psychology'.

| Carl **J** |

4 The Irish author of *Finnegans Wake*.

| James **J** |

5 The lead vocalist of the British 'Rolling Stones' pop group.

| Mick **J** |

6 The first black man to win the world heavyweight boxing championships.

| Jack **J** |

7 An American bank and train robber.

| Jesse **J** |

8 An English author and critic who was a leading figure in 19th-century London literary circles.

| Dr Samuel **J** |

9 The author of *Three Men in a Boat*.

| Jerome K **J** |

10 A Welsh singer whose major hits include 'It's Not Unusual' and 'Green Green Grass Of Home'.

| Tom **J** |

11	Neil Kinnock
12	Charles Kingsley
13	John Knox
14	Rudyard Kipling
15	Martin Luther King
16	Nikita Khrushchev
17	Danny Kaye
18	Grace Kelly
19	Ned Kelly
20	Gene Kelly

11 The British Labour Party leader from 1983 to 1992.

Neil K

12 An English author, best remembered for *The Water Babies*.

Charles K

13 A Scottish religious reformer and founder of the Church of Scotland.

John K

14 The English author of *The Jungle Book*.

Rudyard K

15 A famous American civil rights campaigner who was shot and killed in Memphis in 1968.

Martin Luther K

16 The Russian premier from 1958 to 1964.

Nikita K

17 An American comedian and singer who appeared in films such as *Hans Christian Andersen* and *The Secret Life of Walter Mitty*.

Danny K

18 An American film actress who married Prince Rainier of Monaco.

Grace K

19 A bush Ranger whose exploits have become part of Australian folk lore.

Ned K

20 An American dancer and actor, famous for his 'singin' in the rain' performance.

Gene K

ANSWERS

Musical Films

1 John Travolta

2 Liza Minnelli

3 Shirley Maclaine

4 Barbra Streisand

5 Julie Andrews

6 George Chakiris

7 Rex Harrison

8 Julie Andrews

9 Mitzi Gaynor

10 Elvis Presley

QUESTIONS

Musical Films

 Choose who starred in the musical film named:

1 Grease

- John Travolta ☐
- Cliff Richard ☐
- Madonna ☐

2 Cabaret

- Julie Andrews ☐
- Liza Minnelli ☐
- Bette Midler ☐

3 Sweet Charity

- Petula Clark ☐
- Maggie Smith ☐
- Shirley Maclaine ☐

4 Funny Girl

- Cher ☐
- Rosalind Russell ☐
- Barbra Streisand ☐

5 The Sound of Music

- Audrey Hepburn ☐
- Julie Andrews ☐
- Jean Simmons ☐

6 West Side Story

- Larry Hagman ☐
- John Travolta ☐
- George Chakiris ☐

7 My Fair Lady

- Rex Harrison ☐
- Peter O'Toole ☐
- Peter Finch ☐

8 Mary Poppins

- Julie Andrews ☐
- Susannah York ☐
- Natalie Wood ☐

9 South Pacific

- Deborah Kerr ☐
- Judy Garland ☐
- Mitzi Gaynor ☐

10 Jailhouse Rock

- Tommy Steele ☐
- Elvis Presley ☐
- Bill Haley ☐

ANSWERS

11 Yul Brynner

12 Gordon Macrae

13 Frank Sinatra

14 Bing Crosby

15 Howard Keel

16 Doris Day

17 The Beatles

18 Judy Garland

19 James Cagney

20 Patrick Swayze

11 *The King and I*

Yul Brynner	☐
Charlton Heston	☐
Telly Savalas	☐

12 *Oklahoma*

Rock Hudson	☐
Gordon Macrae	☐
Lee Marvin	☐

13 *Guys and Dolls*

Cary Grant	☐
Noel Coward	☐
Frank Sinatra	☐

14 *White Christmas*

George Sanders	☐
Bob Hope	☐
Bing Crosby	☐

15 *Seven Brides for Seven Brothers*

Gary Cooper	☐
Alan Ladd	☐
Howard Keel	☐

16 *Calamity Jane*

Doris Day	☐
Debbie Reynolds	☐
Betty Hutton	☐

17 *A Hard Day's Night*

The Rolling Stones	☐
Gary Glitter	☐
The Beatles	☐

18 *The Wizard of Oz*

Judy Garland	☐
Elizabeth Taylor	☐
Jane Russell	☐

19 *Yankee Doodle Dandy*

Ray Milland	☐
Edward G Robinson	☐
James Cagney	☐

20 *Dirty Dancing*

Patrick Swayze	☐
Michael York	☐
Dustin Hoffman	☐

ANSWERS

Pot Luck

1 The Alamo

2 Schnozzle

3 The trumpet

4 Pelham

5 Charlie Wilson

6 Barry Humphries

7 Tibet

8 Charles

9 Judy Garland

10 Clint Eastwood

QUESTIONS

Pot Luck

Fill in the answers to the following general knowledge questions about famous people:

1 Davy Crockett died fighting in which battle in 1836?

2 What was the nickname of the comedian, Jimmy Durante?

3 Harry James was renowned for playing which musical instrument?

4 What did the 'P' stand for in the novelist **PG** Wodehouse's name?

5 Who was the former 'Great Train Robber' who was murdered in Marbella in 1990?

6 Who is famous for his impersonation of Dame Edna Everage?

7 The Dalai Lama ruled which country?

8 What was General de Gaulle's first name?

9 Who sang the song 'Over the Rainbow' in the film 'The Wizard of Oz'?

10 Which American actor became a star after making the first spaghetti western 'A Fistful of Dollars'?

ANSWERS

11 Jakob and Wilhelm Grimm

12 The tank

13 Russia

14 Panama

15 Sarah

16 Dan Quayle

17 Mikhail Gorbachev

18 Charles Darwin

19 Golf

20 Katharine Hepburn

QUESTIONS

11 Who were the German brothers who were famous for their collected fairy tales?

12 Sir Ernest Swinton is credited as the inventor of which military machine?

13 Ivan the Terrible ruled which country in the 16th century?

14 General Noriega was dictator of which country?

15 What is the Duchess of York's first name?

16 Who was President George Bush's vice-president?

17 Who did Boris Yeltsin succeed as Soviet president?

18 Which scientist put forward his theory of evolution in *On The Origin of the Species*?

19 In which sport was Tony Jacklin involved?

20 Which actress co-starred with Humphrey Bogart in *The African Queen*?

ANSWERS

People in General

1   China

2   USA

3   Russia

4   China

5   Switzerland

6   France

7   China

8   USA

9   Mexico

10   Brazil

QUESTIONS

People in General

 Which of the three answers given is correct?

1 Which country has the largest population?

China	☐
India	☐
USA	☐

2 Which country has the most university students?

France	☐
China	☐
USA	☐

3 Which country has the most nurses?

Germany	☐
Japan	☐
Russia	☐

4 Which country has the most doctors?

China	☐
USA	☐
Brazil	☐

5 Which country eats the most sweets per person each year?

Britain	☐
Switzerland	☐
USA	☐

6 Which country drinks the most wine per person each year?

France	☐
Italy	☐
Spain	☐

7 Which country has the world's largest army?

USA	☐
China	☐
Iraq	☐

8 Which country has the most people owning cars?

Germany	☐
Japan	☐
USA	☐

9 Which country do the most American tourists visit?

Canada	☐
Britain	☐
Mexico	☐

10 Which country in South America has the largest population?

Brazil	☐
Argentina	☐
Uruguay	☐

11	USA
12	Mexico City
13	Belgium
14	USA
15	Cuba
16	Germany
17	A cigarette butt
18	USA
19	USA
20	Germany

11 Which country has provided the most summer Olympic Games gold medal winners?

USA	☐
Australia	☐
Britain	☐

12 Which city has the world's largest population?

New York	☐
Rio De Janeiro	☐
Mexico City	☐

13 Which country's people consume the most calories of food per person each year?

Italy	☐
Canada	☐
Belgium	☐

14 Which country has the most dentists?

Japan	☐
USA	☐
France	☐

15 Which country's people smoke the most cigarettes each year?

Cuba	☐
Australia	☐
Poland	☐

16 From which country have come the most immigrants to the USA?

Germany	☐
Italy	☐
Ireland	☐

17 In Britain, when people throw litter away, what is it most likely to be?

A sweet wrapper	☐
A cigarette butt	☐
A plastic cup	☐

18 Which country's people make the most telephone calls?

Japan	☐
Britain	☐
USA	☐

19 Which country's people eat the most meat per person each year?

Australia	☐
USA	☐
France	☐

20 Which country's people drink the most beer per person each year?

Australia	☐
Ireland	☐
Germany	☐

1 | **Dr Who**

2 | **Dr Livingstone**

3 | *Dr Zhivago*

4 | **Dr Jekyll**

5 | **James Bond**

6 | **Dr Roger Bannister**

7 | **George Bernard Shaw**

8 | **Dr Stephen Ward**

9 | *Dr Strangelove*

10 | **Leonard McCoy**

Doctors

Fill in the answers to the following general knowledge questions about famous people:

1 Which doctor travelled through time and space in a 'Tardis'?

2 The explorer, Henry Stanley, met which doctor in Africa?

3 Omar Sharif played the title role of a doctor in which 1965 film?

4 Which doctor was the good half of Edward Hyde?

5 *Doctor No* was the first film starring which secret agent?

6 Which medical student, who became a doctor, was the first athlete to break the four-minute mile barrier?

7 Who wrote *The Doctor's Dilemma*?

8 Which doctor was involved in the Profumo sex scandal in 1963?

9 Peter Sellers starred in which 1963 film with a doctor as the title?

10 What was the name of the doctor in the original *Star Trek* TV series?

ANSWERS

11 Dr Watson

12 Dr Dolittle

13 Livesey

14 Dr Samuel Johnson

15 Dr Kildare

16 The Nobel Prize for Medicine

17 W Somerset Maugham

18 Dr Christiaan Barnard

19 Ben Casey

20 Dr Alexander Fleming

QUESTIONS

11 Which doctor was the friend and assistant of Sherlock Holmes?

12 Rex Harrison played which doctor in a 1967 film?

13 What was the surname of the doctor in Robert Louis Stevenson's *Treasure Island*?

14 Which English literary doctor was born in Lichfield, Staffordshire in 1709?

15 Richard Chamberlain played which doctor in a popular British TV series of the 1960s?

16 Dr Emil Behring was the first doctor to win which prize?

17 Which doctor wrote the novels *Of Human Bondage, Cakes and Ale* and *The Moon and Sixpence*?

18 Which South African doctor pioneered heart transplant surgery?

19 Vince Edwards played which doctor in a popular TV series of the 1960s?

20 Which doctor discovered penicillin?

Section 6

Surnames Beginning with L & M

1 **DH Lawrence**

2 **Vivien Leigh**

3 **Jerry Lee Lewis**

4 **Abraham Lincoln**

5 **Jack London**

6 **Sophia Loren**

7 **Niki Lauda**

8 **Charles Lindbergh**

9 **TE Lawrence**

10 **John Lennon**

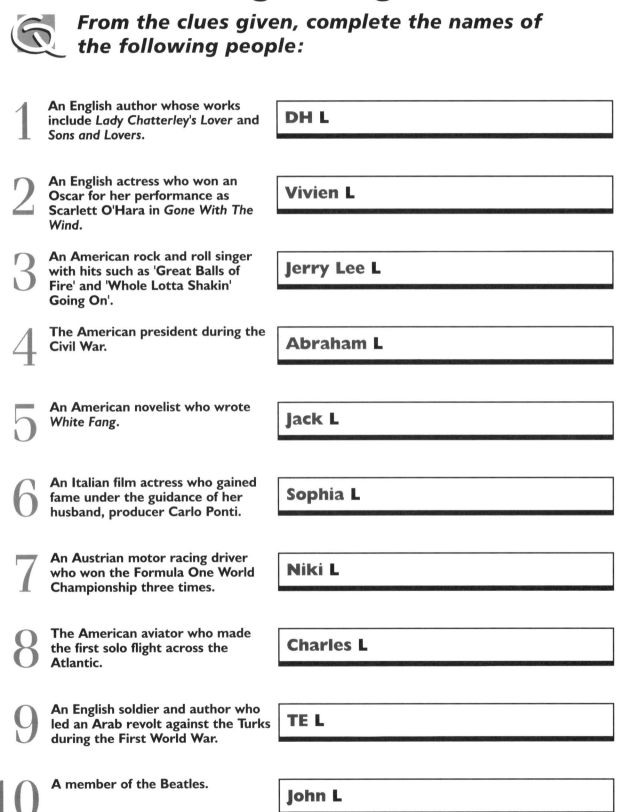

QUESTIONS

Surnames Beginning with L & M

From the clues given, complete the names of the following people:

1 An English author whose works include *Lady Chatterley's Lover* and *Sons and Lovers*.

DH L

2 An English actress who won an Oscar for her performance as Scarlett O'Hara in *Gone With The Wind*.

Vivien L

3 An American rock and roll singer with hits such as 'Great Balls of Fire' and 'Whole Lotta Shakin' Going On'.

Jerry Lee L

4 The American president during the Civil War.

Abraham L

5 An American novelist who wrote *White Fang*.

Jack L

6 An Italian film actress who gained fame under the guidance of her husband, producer Carlo Ponti.

Sophia L

7 An Austrian motor racing driver who won the Formula One World Championship three times.

Niki L

8 The American aviator who made the first solo flight across the Atlantic.

Charles L

9 An English soldier and author who led an Arab revolt against the Turks during the First World War.

TE L

10 A member of the Beatles.

John L

11 Bernard L Montgomery

12 Rupert Murdoch

13 Benito Mussolini

14 Marilyn Monroe

15 Thomas Mann

16 Dudley Moore

17 Golda Meir

18 Walter Matthau

19 Karl Marx

20 Guglielmo Marconi

11 The British field marshal whose victory at El Alamein in 1942 was the turning-point of the war in North Africa.

Bernard L M

12 An Australian entrepreneur and newspaper owner whose business empire spans the globe.

Rupert M

13 The ruler of Italy from 1925 to 1943.

Benito M

14 An American film actress who appeared in such films as *Some Like It Hot* and *The Seven Year Itch*.

Marilyn M

15 The German novelist who wrote the novels *The Magic Mountain* and *Death in Venice*.

Thomas M

16 A British actor and comedian who previously teamed up with Peter Cook.

Dudley M

17 The prime minister of Israel from 1969 to 1974.

Golda M

18 An American character actor, impressive in both comedy and dramatic roles, whose successes include *The Odd Couple* and *Grumpy Old Men*.

Walter M

19 The German philosopher, economist and social theorist who wrote *Das Kapital*.

Karl M

20 The Italian pioneer and inventor in the field of wireless telegraphy.

Guglielmo M

ANSWERS
Comedy

1 Laurel and Hardy

2 Terry Thomas

3 Charlie Chaplin

4 Bob Hope

5 Lee Marvin

6 Dudley Moore

7 George Burns

8 Lucille Ball

9 Buster Keaton

10 Woody Allen

QUESTIONS

Comedy

 Choose the correct humorist/s from the alternatives given:

1 Which comics are associated with the catchphrase 'That's another fine mess you got me in'?

- Laurel and Hardy ☐
- Dean Martin and Jerry Lewis ☐
- Abbott and Costello ☐

2 Who played the baddie in *Those Magnificent Men in Their Flying Machines*?

- David Niven ☐
- Jack Lemmon ☐
- Terry Thomas ☐

3 Who played the Hitler-like part in *The Great Dictator*?

- Buster Keaton ☐
- WC Fields ☐
- Charlie Chaplin ☐

4 Which wise-cracking comedian starred in *The Paleface* and has been honoured with five special Oscars?

- Bob Hope ☐
- Bing Crosby ☐
- Jerry Lewis ☐

5 Who sang 'I was born under a wandrin' star' in the film *Paint Your Wagon*?

- Rock Hudson ☐
- Lee Marvin ☐
- Steve McQueen ☐

6 Who was Peter Cook's comic partner who became a Hollywood star after starring with **Bo Derek** in the film *10*?

- Dudley Moore ☐
- Robin Williams ☐
- Steve Martin ☐

7 Which American cigar chomping comic married Gracie Allen?

- George Burns ☐
- Bill Cosby ☐
- 'Fatty' Arbuckle ☐

8 Which comedy star was married to Desi Arnaz and starred in the TV series *I Love Lucy*?

- Lauren Bacall ☐
- Lucille Ball ☐
- Mary Pickford ☐

9 Who starred with Charlie Chaplin in the film *Limelight*?

- Buster Keaton ☐
- Mel Brooks ☐
- Phil Silvers ☐

10 Which comic film director, actor and screenwriter was married to Mia Farrow?

- Kenneth Branagh ☐
- Woody Allen ☐
- Billy Wilder ☐

ANSWERS

11   **Dustin Hoffman**

12   **John Gielgud**

13   **Noel Coward**

14   **Jack Lemmon**

15   **Rock Hudson**

16   **Peter Sellers**

17   **Tom Selleck**

18   **Danny Kaye**

19   **Buster Keaton**

20   **Jimmy Durante**

QUESTIONS

11 Who was the actor who dressed up as a woman in the film *Tootsie*?

- Tom Cruise ☐
- Patrick Swayze ☐
- Dustin Hoffman ☐

12 Who played the part of the valet in the comedy film *Arthur*?

- Ralph Richardson ☐
- John Gielgud ☐
- Laurence Olivier ☐

13 Who appeared in the comedy thriller *Our Man in Havana*?

- Noel Coward ☐
- Nat King Cole ☐
- Michael Caine ☐

14 In the film *Some Like It Hot* who was Tony Curtis' jazz musician pal?

- Walter Matthau ☐
- Jack Lemmon ☐
- David Niven ☐

15 With whom did Doris Day share a party phone line in the film *Pillow Talk*?

- Cary Grant ☐
- Rock Hudson ☐
- Gregory Peck ☐

16 Who played the part of a French policeman in the film *The Pink Panther*?

- Cesar Romero ☐
- Claude Rains ☐
- Peter Sellers ☐

17 Who appeared in the film *Three Men and a Baby*?

- Tom Selleck ☐
- Kevin Costner ☐
- Richard Gere ☐

18 Who starred in the films *The Secret Life of Walter Mitty* and *The Court Jester*?

- Bing Crosby ☐
- Gene Kelly ☐
- Danny Kaye ☐

19 Which comedy actor was named *The Great Stone Face*?

- Buster Keaton ☐
- Cary Grant ☐
- WC Fields ☐

20 Which comedian with a gravel voice was known by the nickname 'Schnozzola' and always ended his act with the line 'Goodnight, Mrs Calabash, wherever you are'?

- Phil Silvers ☐
- Jimmy Durante ☐
- 'Fatty' Arbuckle ☐

1   **The Chancellor of the Exchequer**

2   **Painting and sculpture**

3   **Leonard Bernstein**

4   **Lionel Bart**

5   **Michaelangelo**

6   **Methuselah**

7   **Robert Browning
('Home Thoughts from Abroad')**

8   **Peter Falk**

9   **Edward Heath**

10 **Roy Orbison**

QUESTIONS

Pot Luck

Fill in the answers to the following general knowledge questions about famous people:

1 Who lives at No. 11 Downing Street?

2 What was Salvador Dali famous for?

3 Who composed the music for the film *West Side Story*?

4 Who wrote the music for the hit musical 'Oliver'?

5 Who was the great painter who also sculpted the statue **David** in Florence?

6 Who is the oldest man in the Bible?

7 Who wrote the poem that begins: 'Oh to be in England, Now that April's there...'?

8 Who played the detective Colombo in the television series of the same name?

9 Which politician is associated with the yacht *Morning Cloud*?

10 Which pop star had hits with 'Only the Lonely' and 'Pretty Woman'?

11 Richard Nixon

12 Mary Wilson

13 Liberace

14 George Orwell

15 Joseph Stalin

16 Labour

17 *Coronation Street*

18 Johnny Weissmuller

19 Children's books

20 Ice skating

QUESTIONS

11 Which American president said: 'There will be no whitewash at the White House'?

12 Which British prime minister's wife published a volume of her own poems?

13 Which popular American pianist always had a candelabra on his piano?

14 Who wrote the novels *Keep the Aspidistra Flying* and *Animal Farm*?

15 Which Soviet ruler had a daughter called Svetlana?

16 Which political party did George Brown belong to?

17 In which television series is Ken Barlow a key character?

18 Which great American swimmer became famous for his portrayal of Tarzan in 19 films?

19 What sort of books did Enid Blyton write?

20 What did John Curry do to become well known?

ANSWERS
Inventors

1 **Television**

2 **Parking meter**

3 **The powered aeroplane**

4 **Bouncing bomb**

5 **Safety razor**

6 **Combine harvester**

7 **Telephone**

8 **Disc brakes**

9 **Aqualung**

10 **Electric light bulb**

QUESTIONS

Inventors

 Which one of the alternatives given did the person named invent?

1 John Logie Baird

Television	☐
Electric kettle	☐
Motorcycle	☐

2 Carlton Magee

Bicycle pump	☐
Traffic lights	☐
Parking meter	☐

3 Wilbur and Orville Wright

Submarine	☐
Railway engine	☐
Powered aeroplane	☐

4 Sir Barnes Wallis

Bouncing bomb	☐
Laser	☐
Radar	☐

5 King Camp Gillette

Safety razor	☐
Safety match	☐
Safety pin	☐

6 Benjamin Holt

Tractor	☐
Combine harvester	☐
Bulldozer	☐

7 Alexander Graham Bell

Juke box	☐
Telephone	☐
Walkman	☐

8 Dr F Lanchester

Carburettor	☐
Fuel pump	☐
Disc brakes	☐

9 Jacques Cousteau

Aqualung	☐
Submarine	☐
Flippers	☐

10 Thomas Edison

Microscope	☐
Electric light bulb	☐
Loud speaker	☐

11 | **Frozen food**

12 | **Lie detector**

13 | **Electric razor**

14 | **Launderette**

15 | **Stainless steel**

16 | **Radio**

17 | **Jet engine**

18 | **Hydrofoil**

19 | **Cellophane**

20 | **Shorthand**

11 Clarence Birdseye

- Ice cream ☐
- Frozen food ☐
- Ice bucket ☐

12 John A Larson

- Microphone ☐
- Lie detector ☐
- Radar ☐

13 Jacob Schick

- Electric razor ☐
- Electric kettle ☐
- Electric toothbrush ☐

14 JF Cantrell

- Launderette ☐
- Pizza parlour ☐
- Sauna bath ☐

15 Harry Brearly

- Polythene ☐
- Stainless steel ☐
- Rubber tyres ☐

16 Guglielmo Marconi

- Radio ☐
- Electric sunroof ☐
- Tubeless tyres ☐

17 Sir Frank Whittle

- Electric engine ☐
- Steam engine ☐
- Jet engine ☐

18 Enrico Forlamini

- Hovercraft ☐
- Submarine ☐
- Hydrofoil ☐

19 Jacques Brandenberger

- Writing paper ☐
- Polythene ☐
- Cellophane ☐

20 Sir Isaac Pitman

- Printing press ☐
- Typewriter ☐
- Shorthand ☐

Nicknames

1 **Robert Burns**

2 **Mary I or Mary Tudor**

3 **Richard I**

4 **Stonewall Jackson**

5 **Jack Dempsey**

6 **Rod Laver**

7 **General Patton**

8 **Lawrence of Arabia**

9 **Helen of Troy**

10 **Bonnie Prince Charlie**

128   **Quiz Book for Groups: Famous People**

Nicknames

Fill in the answers to the following general knowledge questions about famous people:

1 Which poet was known as 'The Bard of Ayrshire'?

2 'Bloody Mary' was the name given to which English queen?

3 Which English king was called 'Lionheart'?

4 What was the nickname given to the American Confederate general Thomas Jonathan Jackson?

5 'The Manassa Mauler' was the name given to which world heavyweight champion boxer?

6 Which Australian tennis champion became known as the 'Rockhampton Rocket'?

7 Which American Second World War general was known as 'Old Blood and Guts'?

8 By what other name was TE Lawrence renowned?

9 Who had 'the face that launched a thousand ships'?

10 Prince Charles Edward Stuart was known as 'The Young Pretender', but what was his more familiar nickname?

11	Joan of Arc

12	Charles Lindbergh

13	Louis Armstrong

14	William Shakespeare

15	The Duke of Wellington

16	Prince Otto Eduard Leopold von Bismarck

17	Joe Louis

18	The Red Baron

19	Esther Williams

20	Lord Lucan

11 Who was the 'Maid of Orleans'?

12 Which famous aviator was known as 'The Lone Aviator'?

13 What was the musician 'Satchmo's' real name?

14 Which famous playwright was 'The Bard of Avon'?

15 Who was the 'Iron Duke'?

16 Who was the 'Iron Chancellor'?

17 Which heavyweight boxing champion was called 'The Brown Bomber'?

18 What other name was given to Baron Von Richthofen?

19 Which American actress was known as 'Hollywood's Mermaid'?

20 Which English lord who became a fugitive was nicknamed 'Lucky'?

Section 7

Surnames Beginning with N & O

1   **Ivor Novello**

2   **Alfred Nobel**

3   **David Niven**

4   **Florence Nightingale**

5   **Richard M Nixon**

6   **Edith Nesbit**

7   **Paul Newman**

8   **Horatio Nelson**

9   **Gamal Abdel Nasser**

10   **Martina Navratilova**

QUESTIONS

Surnames Beginning with N & O

From the clues given, complete the names of the following people:

1   A Welsh composer of popular songs such as 'Keep The Home Fires Burning'.

Ivor **N**

2   The Swedish chemist and inventor of dynamite who left a large fortune for endowment of prizes named after him.

Alfred **N**

3   A Scots-born British actor whose films included the Oscar-winning *Separate Tables*.

David **N**

4   She became known as the lady of the lamp and for her reforms of the nursing profession.

Florence **N**

5   The 37th President of the USA who resigned in 1974 over the Watergate affair.

Richard M **N**

6   The author of *The Railway Children*.

Edith **N**

7   An American actor and director whose films include *The Hustler* and *Butch Cassidy and the Sundance Kid*.

Paul **N**

8   A famous English admiral who was killed at Trafalgar.

Horatio **N**

9   The president of Egypt from 1956 to 1970.

Gamal Abdel **N**

10   The most outstanding female tennis player of the 1980s, who won nine singles titles.

Martina **N**

ANSWERS

11 Jesse Owens

12 Peter O'Toole

13 David Owen

14 Roy Orbison

15 Baroness Orczy

16 Steve Ovett

17 George Orwell

18 Aristotle Onassis

19 Sir Laurence Olivier

20 Donny Osmond

11 An American track and field athlete who won four gold medals in the 1936 Olympics and held the long jump world record for 25 years.

Jesse O

12 A British actor who made his name in the 1962 film, *Lawrence of Arabia*.

Peter O

13 A British politician who was a founder member of the Social Democrat Party (SDP).

David O

14 An American singer, who died in 1988, who was famous for such songs as 'Only The Lonely' and 'Pretty Woman'.

Roy O

15 The Hungarian-born novelist who wrote *The Scarlet Pimpernel*.

Baroness O

16 A British athlete who won an Olympic gold medal in the 800 metres and also held the 1500 metre world record.

Steve O

17 The author of *1984*.

George O

18 The shipping magnate who married the widow of John F Kennedy.

Aristotle O

19 An English actor and director who, for many years, was associated with the Old Vic.

Sir Laurence O

20 An American singer who was a member of a chart-topping family pop group in the 1970s.

Donny O

Famous Partners

1 | Jeannette McDonald

2 | Bob Geldof

3 | Fred Astaire

4 | Hugh Laurie

5 | Elizabeth Taylor

6 | John Lennon

7 | Laurence Olivier

8 | Lou Costello

9 | Christopher Dean

10 | Dean Martin

QUESTIONS

Famous Partners

 Can you identify from the three choices given who was or is the partner of each of the following famous people?

1 Nelson Eddy

Rita Hayworth	☐
Jeannette McDonald	☐
Betty Grable	☐

2 Paula Yates

Bob Geldof	☐
Bill Wyman	☐
Keith Richards	☐

3 Ginger Rogers

Gene Kelly	☐
Danny Kaye	☐
Fred Astaire	☐

4 Stephen Fry

Hugh Laurie	☐
John Cleese	☐
Rowan Atkinson	☐

5 Richard Burton

Rita Hayworth	☐
Elizabeth Taylor	☐
Jane Fonda	☐

6 Yoko Ono

John Lennon	☐
Mick Jagger	☐
Rod Stewart	☐

7 Vivien Leigh

Laurence Olivier	☐
Gregory Peck	☐
Trevor Howard	☐

8 Bud Abbott

Bob Hope	☐
Buster Keaton	☐
Lou Costello	☐

9 Jayne Torvill

Christopher Dean	☐
John Curry	☐
Robin Cousins	☐

10 Jerry Lewis

Frank Sinatra	☐
Dean Martin	☐
Lee Marvin	☐

ANSWERS

11 Katharine Hepburn

12 Cher

13 Dudley Moore

14 Sullivan

15 Oliver Hardy

16 Oscar Hammerstein II

17 Rudolph Nureyev

18 Anne Hathaway

19 Miss Piggy

20 Garfunkel

11 Spencer Tracy

Bette Davis ☐

Katharine Hepburn ☐

Joan Crawford ☐

12 Sonny

Prince ☐

Garfunkel ☐

Cher ☐

13 Peter Cook

Mike Yarwood ☐

Dudley Moore ☐

Bernie Winters ☐

14 Gilbert

Porter ☐

Sullivan ☐

Styne ☐

15 Stan Laurel

Charlie Chaplin ☐

WC Fields ☐

Oliver Hardy ☐

16 Richard Rodgers

Oscar Hammerstein II ☐

Irving Berlin ☐

George Gershwin ☐

17 Margot Fonteyn

Vaslaw Nijinsky ☐

Rudolph Nureyev ☐

Leonide Massine ☐

18 William Shakespeare

Jane Austen ☐

Anne Hathaway ☐

George Eliot ☐

19 Kermit

Sylvester ☐

Miss Piggy ☐

Woodstock ☐

20 Simon

Garfunkel ☐

Frederick ☐

Bono ☐

ANSWERS

Pot Luck

1 Peter Sellers

2 Theodore (Teddy) Roosevelt

3 Marie Antoinette

4 Frederick Forsyth

5 Pythagoras

6 Chess

7 Sir Walter Raleigh

8 Sir Francis Drake

9 Tonto

10 Enid Blyton

QUESTIONS

Pot Luck

Fill in the answers to the following general knowledge questions about famous people:

1 Which British actor played Inspector Clouseau in the 'Pink Panther' films?

2 After which American president was the teddy bear named?

3 Which queen of France was guillotined during the French Revolution?

4 Who wrote the novels *The Day of the Jackal* and *The Odessa File*?

5 Which Greek mathematician had a theorem about the squares on the three sides of a right-angled triangle?

6 What game did Bobby Fischer become famous for playing?

7 Who is reputed to have introduced potatoes into Britain?

8 Who is believed to be the first Englishman to sail round the world?

9 Who was the Lone Ranger's helper?

10 Which children's author wrote about 'The Secret Seven' and 'The Famous Five'.

A A A A A A A A A A A A A A A A A A A A

ANSWERS

11 Mowgli

12 Richard Harris

13 Pablo Picasso

14 Indira Gandhi

15 General Charles de Gaulle

16 Richard Strauss

17 David Niven

18 Lewis Carroll

19 Joseph

20 Canada

A A A A A A A A A A A A A A A A A A A A

144   Quiz Book for Groups: Famous People

11 Who was the Indian boy in Rudyard Kipling's *Jungle Book?*

12 Who was the Irish-born actor who starred in the films *The Wild Geese* and *A Man Called Horse?*

13 Which great painter had a blue period?

14 Which woman became prime minister of India in 1966?

15 Who founded the Free French movement during the Second World War?

16 Who composed 'Der Rosenkavalier'?

17 Who played the part of Phileas Fogg in the film *Around the World in Eighty Days?*

18 Who wrote *Alice's Adventures in Wonderland* and *Through the Looking-Glass?*

19 In the Bible, who had a coat of many colours?

20 Of which country did Pierre Trudeau become prime minister?

1 **Shirley Maclaine**

2 **Hannibal**

3 **Lionel Barrymore**

4 **Ira Gershwin**

5 **Richard I**

6 **James Fox**

7 **Sally Oldfield**

8 **Loretta Lynn**

9 **Princess Margaret**

10 **Julian Lloyd Webber**

QUESTIONS

Brothers, Sisters and Cousins

 Decide who is related to whom:

1 Warren Beatty's famous sister is:

Raquel Welch	☐
Elizabeth Taylor	☐
Shirley Maclaine	☐

2 Hasdrubal was the brother of:

Cleopatra	☐
Hannibal	☐
Nero	☐

3 Ethel and John Barrymore's famous brother was called:

Arthur	☐
David	☐
Lionel	☐

4 George Gershwin's brother was called:

Peter	☐
Ira	☐
Enoch	☐

5 King John of England was the brother of:

Henry I	☐
Richard I	☐
Edward I	☐

6 The English actor Edward Fox's brother, also in the acting profession, is called:

Peter	☐
David	☐
James	☐

7 The sister of rock musician Mike Oldfield is named:

Sally	☐
Ann	☐
Shirley	☐

8 Crystal Gayle's country singing sister is:

Loretta Lynn	☐
Dolly Parton	☐
Reba McEntire	☐

9 Queen Elizabeth II's sister is:

Princess Margaret	☐
Princess Anne	☐
Princess Aurora	☐

10 The brother of the composer Andrew Lloyd Webber is called:

Edward	☐
Tony	☐
Julian	☐

11	**Napoleon Bonaparte**

12	**Ernie Tyrell**

13	**Bobby Charlton**

14	**Attila the Hun**

15	**Olivia de Havilland**

16	**George V**

17	**David Niven**

18	**Mary Queen of Scots**

19	**Ian Fleming**

20	**Sherlock Holmes**

11 Joseph and Louis were the names of the brothers of:

General De Gaulle	☐
Maurice Chevalier	☐
Napoleon Bonaparte	☐

12 A member of the Supremes pop group was a sister of the boxer:

Muhammad Ali	☐
Archie Moore	☐
Ernie Tyrell	☐

13 The Irish football team manager, Jack Charlton, has a brother named:

Bobby	☐
Gazza	☐
Harry	☐

14 Bleda was the brother of:

Attila the Hun	☐
Genghis Khan	☐
William Tell	☐

15 The actress, Joan Fontaine, is the sister of:

Vivien Leigh	☐
Olivia de Havilland	☐
Marilyn Monroe	☐

16 The British king who was a cousin of Kaiser Wilhelm of Germany was:

Edward VII	☐
George IV	☐
George V	☐

17 Patrick MacNee, known for his role in the TV show *The Avengers*, had a famous film star cousin called:

Peter Finch	☐
David Niven	☐
Gary Cooper	☐

18 The cousin of Elizabeth I was:

Mary Queen of Scots	☐
Anne of Cleves	☐
Jane Seymour	☐

19 The author cousin of the horror film star Christopher Lee was:

George Orwell	☐
Somerset Maugham	☐
Ian Fleming	☐

20 Mycroft was the brother of the fictional detective:

Sherlock Holmes	☐
Kojak	☐
Hercule Poirot	☐

ANSWERS

Novels and Novelists

1 | Billy Bunter

2 | Quasimodo

3 | JRR Tolkien

4 | Nicholas Monsarrat

5 | Rhett Butler (*Gone with the Wind*)

6 | PD James

7 | *Lorna Doone*

8 | The Three Musketeers

9 | Ruth Rendell

10 | *Wuthering Heights*

Novels and Novelists

Fill in the answers to the following general knowledge questions about famous people:

1 Who was the fattest pupil at Greyfriars School?

2 What was the name of the hunchback of Notre Dame?

3 Who wrote *The Hobbit* and *Lord of the Rings*?

4 Who wrote *The Cruel Sea*?

5 Which fictional character said: "Frankly, my dear, I don't give a damn"?

6 Who created the detective, Commander Adam Dalgliesh?

7 In which novel is John Rudd the central male character?

8 'All for one and one for all' is the motto of which fictional characters?

9 By what other name is the crime writer Barbara Vine known?

10 In which novel was Heathcliff a key character?

ANSWERS

11 Dick Francis

12 Mary Shelley

13 Mark Twain

14 Miss Moneypenny

15 Kingsley Amis

16 Daphne Du Maurier

17 Science fiction

18 Jeffrey Archer

19 James Joyce

20 HG Wells

11 Which famous jockey writes crime novels?

12 Who wrote the gothic novel *Frankenstein*?

13 Which author said: "Reports of my death are greatly exaggerated"?

14 What is the name of 'M's secretary in the James Bond novels?

15 Which author became popular with his novel *Lucky Jim* and has a son called Martin who also writes novels?

16 What author wrote a novel about *Jamaica Inn*?

17 What sort of novels did Arthur C Clarke become famous for writing?

18 Who wrote the novels *Kane and Abel* and *First Among Equals*?

19 Which Irish author wrote *Ulysses* and *Finnegans Wake*?

20 Who wrote *The History of Mr Polly*, *The Time Machine* and *Kipps*?

Section 8

ANSWERS

Surnames Beginning with P & R

1 Niccolo Paganini

2 Vincent Price

3 Alain Prost

4 Emmeline Pankhurst

5 Catherine Parr

6 Boris Pasternak

7 Charlie Parker

8 Luciano Pavarotti

9 Lester Piggott

10 Evita Peron

Surnames Beginning with *P & R*

From the clues given, complete the names of the following people:

1   An Italian composer famous for his works for the violin.

   Niccolo P

2   A famous American horror film star.

   Vincent P

3   A French motor racing driver who has won the Formula One World championship four times.

   Alain P

4   A campaigner for women's rights.

   Emmeline P

5   The sixth wife of King Henry VIII of England.

   Catherine P

6   A Russian Poet and novelist whose best known work is *Dr Zhivago*.

   Boris P

7   An American jazz musician who was nicknamed 'Bird'.

   Charlie P

8   A famous Italian tenor who was born in 1935.

   Luciano P

9   The English champion jockey who rode a record nine Derby winners.

   Lester P

10 An Argentinian populist leader born in Buenos Aires who was involved in the government of her husband Juan.

   Evita P

ANSWERS

11 Yitzhak Rabin

12 Grigori Rasputin

13 Robert Runcie

14 Ronald Reagan

15 Robert Redford

16 Erno Rubik

17 Pierre-Auguste Renoir

18 Cecil Rhodes

19 Erwin Rommel

20 Roy Rogers

11   He succeeded Golda Meir as prime minister of Israel in 1974.

Yitzhak **R**

12   A Siberian 'holy man' who gained an influence over the Russian royal family in the early 20th century.

Grigori **R**

13   The English cleric who became the Archbishop of Canterbury in 1980.

Robert **R**

14   The president of the USA from 1981 to 1989.

Ronald **R**

15   An American film actor and director whose first starring role was in *Butch Cassidy and the Sundance Kid*.

Robert **R**

16   The Hungarian inventor of a popular cube.

Erno **R**

17   A French impressionist artist whose works included *La Loge* and *The Umbrellas*.

Pierre-Auguste **R**

18   A 19th-century South African politician who was the founder of Rhodesia.

Cecil **R**

19   A Second World War German field marshal known as 'The Desert Fox'.

Erwin **R**

20   A famous singing cowboy who had a horse named Trigger.

Roy **R**

ANSWERS

Oscar-Winning Actors

1 | **Dustin Hoffman**

2 | **Gary Cooper**

3 | **Marlon Brando**

4 | **George C Scott**

5 | **Lee Marvin**

6 | **Burt Lancaster**

7 | **Alec Guinness**

8 | **Marlon Brando**

9 | **Henry Fonda**

10 | **Jack Lemmon**

QUESTIONS

Oscar-Winning Actors

 Which of the three given actors won an Oscar for the film named?

1 *Kramer vs Kramer*

Jon Voight	☐
Henry Fonda	☐
Dustin Hoffman	☐

2 *High Noon*

John Wayne	☐
Gary Cooper	☐
Alan Ladd	☐

3 *The Godfather*

Gene Hackman	☐
Rod Steiger	☐
Marlon Brando	☐

4 *Patton*

George C Scott	☐
Paul Newman	☐
Gregory Peck	☐

5 *Cat Ballou*

Clint Eastwood	☐
Lee Marvin	☐
Rock Hudson	☐

6 *Elmer Gantry*

Burt Lancaster	☐
Kirk Douglas	☐
Spencer Tracy	☐

7 *Bridge on the River Kwai*

Alec Guinness	☐
David Niven	☐
Edward Fox	☐

8 *On the Waterfront*

Clark Gable	☐
James Mason	☐
Marlon Brando	☐

9 *On Golden Pond*

Spencer Tracy	☐
Henry Fonda	☐
William Holden	☐

10 *Save the Tiger*

Jack Lemmon	☐
Walter Matthau	☐
Tony Curtis	☐

11 Ben Kingsley

12 Paul Schofield

13 Charlton Heston

14 Daniel Day-Lewis

15 Paul Newman

16 Rex Harrison

17 Gene Hackman

18 Humphrey Bogart

19 John Wayne

20 Yul Brynner

QUESTIONS

11 *Gandhi*

David Niven	☐
Ben Kingsley	☐
Edward Fox	☐

12 *A Man for All Seasons*

Paul Schofield	☐
Peter O'Toole	☐
Ralph Richardson	☐

13 *Ben-Hur*

Burt Lancaster	☐
Kirk Douglas	☐
Charlton Heston	☐

14 *My Left Foot*

Jeremy Irons	☐
John Hurt	☐
Daniel Day-Lewis	☐

15 *The Color of Money*

Robert Redford	☐
Paul Newman	☐
Dustin Hoffman	☐

16 *My Fair Lady*

Rex Harrison	☐
David Niven	☐
Trevor Howard	☐

17 *The French Connection*

Kevin Costner	☐
Walter Matthau	☐
Gene Hackman	☐

18 *The African Queen*

Peter Lorre	☐
Humphrey Bogart	☐
James Cagney	☐

19 *True Grit*

Dean Martin	☐
John Wayne	☐
Clint Eastwood	☐

20 *The King and I*

Yul Brynner	☐
Ernest Borgnine	☐
William Holden	☐

ANSWERS

Pot Luck

1 Martin Luther King

2 *The Magic Roundabout*

3 Tennis

4 Andrew Lloyd Webber

5 Cliff Richard

6 Lester Piggott

7 Shirley Bassey

8 Elvis Presley

9 Sculpture

10 Harold Macmillan

Pot Luck

Fill in the answers to the following general knowledge questions about famous people:

1   Which civil rights leader did James Earl Ray shoot in Memphis, Tennessee in 1968?

2   In which television series do Dougal, Florence and Zebedee take part?

3   Billie Jean King was famous for which sport?

4   Who composed the music for the musical show *Cats*?

5   Which pop singer starred in the film *Summer Holiday*?

6   Who was the champion jockey who went to prison in 1987?

7   Who sang the title song for the James Bond film, *Goldfinger*?

8   Which pop star did Colonel Tom Parker manage?

9   Barbara Hepworth was famous for which art?

10   Which British prime minister told his electors that they had "never had it so good"?

ANSWERS

11 Roald Amundsen

12 Richard Adams

13 Amy Johnson

14 Oscar Wilde

15 Conservative

16 Charlton Heston

17 Telly Savalas

18 Margaret Thatcher

19 Samson

20 William Wordsworth

QUESTIONS

11   Who is credited with being the first man to reach the South Pole?

12   Who wrote the novel *Watership Down?*

13   Who was the first woman to fly solo from England to Australia?

14   Who wrote the play *The Importance of Being Ernest?*

15   To which political party did Sir Anthony Eden belong?

16   Who played the part of Judah Ben-Hur in the film *Ben-Hur?*

17   Who played the detective Kojak in the television series of the same name?

18   Who said: "I've got a woman's ability to stick to a job and get on with it when everyone else walks off and leaves it"?

19   Which biblical character lost his strength when his hair was cut off?

20   Which poet wrote the poem 'I Wandered Lonely' commonly known as 'The Daffodils'?

Famous Last Words

1   **Lord Nelson**

2   **Mary Tudor**

3   **Oscar Wilde**

4   **Beethoven**

5   **Douglas Fairbanks Snr**

6   **Julius Caesar**

7   **King George V**

8   **Elizabeth I**

9   **Ned Kelly**

10   **HG Wells**

QUESTIONS

Famous Last Words

To whom are the following last words attributed?

1 "Thank God I have done my duty."

Oliver Cromwell	☐
Lord Byron	☐
Lord Nelson	☐

2 "When I am dead and opened, you shall find Calais lying in my heart."

Mary Tudor	☐
Lord Byron	☐
General de Gaulle	☐

3 "Either that wallpaper goes, or I do."

Napoleon III	☐
Queen Victoria	☐
Oscar Wilde	☐

4 "I shall hear in heaven."

Beethoven	☐
Mozart	☐
Tchaikovsky	☐

5 "I've never felt better."

Douglas Fairbanks Snr	☐
Humphrey Bogart	☐
James Cagney	☐

6 "Et tu, Brute."

Nero	☐
Caligula	☐
Julius Caesar	☐

7 "How is the Empire?"

King George V	☐
Winston Churchill	☐
Queen Victoria	☐

8 "All my possessions but for one moment of time."

Elizabeth I	☐
Richard III	☐
Henry VIII	☐

9 "Such is life."

John Dillinger	☐
Al Capone	☐
Ned Kelly	☐

10 "Go away, I'm all right."

Jules Verne	☐
HG Wells	☐
Somerset Maugham	☐

ANSWERS

11   Queen Victoria

12   Mahler

13   Karl Marx

14   Lord Palmerston

15   Charles II

16   Vincent Van Gogh

17   Dylan Thomas

18   Humphrey Bogart

19   Richard III

20   Captain Lawrence Oates

QUESTIONS

11 "Oh that peace may come."

Duke of Wellington ☐
David Lloyd George ☐
Queen Victoria ☐

12 "Mozart!"

Tchaikovsky ☐
Debussy ☐
Mahler ☐

13 "Last words are for fools who haven't said enough."

Karl Marx ☐
General de Gaulle ☐
Theodore Roosevelt ☐

14 "Die, my dear Watson? Why that's the last thing I shall do."

Duke of Wellington ☐
Prince Albert ☐
Lord Palmerston ☐

15 "Let not poor Nelly starve."

Charles II ☐
Henry II ☐
Edward II ☐

16 "I shall never get rid of this depression."

Picasso ☐
Leonardo Da Vinci ☐
Vincent Van Gogh ☐

17 "I've had 18 straight whiskies, I think that's a record."

Thomas Hardy ☐
Dylan Thomas ☐
George Orwell ☐

18 "I should never have switched from scotch to Martini."

Humphrey Bogart ☐
Errol Flynn ☐
Clark Gable ☐

19 "Treason! Treason!"

Charles I ☐
Edward II ☐
Richard III ☐

20 "I am just going outside and I may be gone some time."

Captain Lawrence Oates ☐
Captain Edward Smith ☐
General William Sherman ☐

1   Prince Philip (Duke of Edinburgh)

2   Queen Elizabeth the Queen Mother

3   Princess Anne

4   Wallis Simpson

5   His investiture as the Prince of Wales

6   The Queen Mother

7   Prince Philip (Duke of Edinburgh)

8   Mark Phillips

9   Winston Churchill

10   Prince Andrew

QUESTIONS

Royalty

Fill in the answers to the following general knowledge questions about famous people:

1 Which member of the royal family was born in Greece?

2 Who lives in Clarence House?

3 Who is president of the Save the Children Fund?

4 Who did Edward VIII abdicate his throne to marry?

5 What happened to Prince Charles on 1 July 1969 at Caernarfon Castle in Wales?

6 After King George VI's death in 1952, what was his wife called?

7 Which member of the royal family said: "I never see any home cooking. All I get is fancy stuff."

8 Who did Princess Anne marry on 14 November 1973?

9 Who was prime minister when Elizabeth II came to the throne?

10 Which of Elizabeth II's children was born on 19 February 1960.

11   Princess Anne

12   Prince Andrew

13   Princess Margaret

14   Spencer

15   Prince Edward

16   George V

17   Beatrice and Eugenie

18   George VI

19   Princess Margaret

20   Prince Albert

11 Who was shot at, in an unsuccessful kidnap attempt, in **The Mall**, in March 1974?

12 Which member of the royal family served in the navy during the Falklands war?

13 Whom did Antony Armstrong-Jones marry?

14 What was the surname of the Princess of Wales before she married Prince Charles?

15 What is the name of Queen Elizabeth II's youngest son?

16 Which king reigned in Britain at the start of the First World War?

17 What are the names of the Duke of York's two daughters?

18 To which king was Lady Elizabeth Bowes-Lyon married?

19 Roddy Llewellyn was a close friend of which princess?

20 Who was Queen Victoria's husband?

Section 9

Surnames Beginning with S & T

1 | Sylvester Stallone

2 | John Steinbeck

3 | Jackie Stewart

4 | Barbra Streisand

5 | Anna Sewell

6 | Robert Falcon Scott

7 | Franz Schubert

8 | Helmut Schmidt

9 | Jean-Paul Sartre

10 | Dorothy L Sayers

Surnames Beginning with S & T

From the clues given, complete the names of the following people:

1 An American film star who made his name in the 'Rocky' films.

Sylvester **S**

2 An American author whose works include *The Grapes of Wrath* and *Of Mice and Men*.

John **S**

3 A Scots Formula One world champion who held the record for the most grand prix wins until surpassed by Alain Prost in 1987.

Jackie **S**

4 An American singer, actress and film director who starred in *Funny Girl* and *A Star is Born*.

Barbra **S**

5 The author of *Black Beauty*.

Anna **S**

6 The leader of the second expedition to reach the south pole, who died on the return journey.

Robert Falcon **S**

7 The Austrian composer of *The Unfinished Symphony*.

Franz **S**

8 The chancellor of West Germany from 1974 to 1982.

Helmut **S**

9 A French author and philosopher who was one of the leading proponents of existentialism.

Jean-Paul **S**

10 The creator of the aristocratic detective, Lord Peter Wimsey.

Dorothy L **S**

ANSWERS

11 Pyotr Ilyich Tchaikovsky

12 William Makepeace Thackeray

13 Leon Trotsky

14 Tina Turner

15 Leo Tolstoy

16 Dylan Thomas

17 Harry S Truman

18 Desmond Tutu

19 Mike Tyson

20 Dick Turpin

11 A famous Russian composer whose ballets include *The Sleeping Beauty* and *The Nutcracker*.

Pyotr Ilyich **T**

12 The English author of *Vanity Fair*.

William Makepeace **T**

13 A leading Russian revolutionary who was assassinated in Mexico in 1940.

Leon **T**

14 An American rhythm and blues-based singer who recorded with her husband Ike and then embarked on a highly successful solo career.

Tina **T**

15 The Russian author of *War and Peace*.

Leo **T**

16 A Welsh poet and author whose best known work is *Under Milk Wood*.

Dylan **T**

17 President of the USA from 1945 to 1953.

Harry S **T**

18 The South African archbishop who won the Nobel Peace Prize in 1984.

Desmond **T**

19 The undisputed world heavyweight boxing champion from 1987 to 1990.

Mike **T**

20 An infamous English highwayman who was hanged in 1739.

Dick **T**

Marriages

1 George of Denmark

2 Greg Allman

3 Joan Crawford

4 Agatha Christie

5 Charlie Chaplin

6 Mozart

7 Carole Lombard

8 Mary Queen of Scots

9 Robert Louis Stevenson

10 Eddie Fisher

QUESTIONS

Marriages

 Choose from the alternatives given to whom the following persons have been or are married:

1 Queen Anne of Britain

George of Denmark	☐
Henry of Portugal	☐
Louis of Spain	☐

2 Cher

Duane Eddy	☐
Greg Allman	☐
Dustin Hoffman	☐

3 Douglas Fairbanks Jnr

Bette Davis	☐
Betty Grable	☐
Joan Crawford	☐

4 Sir Max Mallowan

Dorothy L Sayers	☐
Agatha Christie	☐
Daphne Du Maurier	☐

5 Paulette Goddard

Errol Flynn	☐
Charlie Chaplin	☐
James Cagney	☐

6 Constanze Weber

Schubert	☐
Wagner	☐
Mozart	☐

7 Clark Gable

Betty Grable	☐
Vivien Leigh	☐
Carole Lombard	☐

8 Lord Darnley and the Earl of Bothwell

Mary Tudor	☐
Mary Queen of Scots	☐
Queen Mary II	☐

9 Fanny Osbourne

William Wordsworth	☐
John Keats	☐
Robert Louis Stevenson	☐

10 Debbie Reynolds

Dean Martin	☐
Eddie Fisher	☐
Burt Lancaster	☐

ANSWERS

11 Mao Tse-tung

12 Ronald Reagan

13 Ava Gardner

14 Frank Sinatra

15 Elliott Gould

16 Rita Hayworth

17 Richard I

18 Blake Edwards

19 Conrad Hilton

20 Demi Moore

11 Chiang Ch'ing

Mao Tse-tung	☐
Sun Yat-sen	☐
Bruce Lee	☐

12 Jane Wyman

Jimmy Carter	☐
Richard Nixon	☐
Ronald Reagan	☐

13 Mickey Rooney

Vivien Leigh	☐
Ava Gardner	☐
Olivia de Havilland	☐

14 Ava Gardner

Dean Martin	☐
Tony Bennett	☐
Frank Sinatra	☐

15 Barbra Streisand

Elliott Gould	☐
Peter Sellers	☐
Robert Redford	☐

16 Orson Welles

Lana Turner	☐
Jayne Mansfield	☐
Rita Hayworth	☐

17 Queen Beregaria

Richard I	☐
Richard II	☐
Richard III	☐

18 Julie Andrews

Blake Edwards	☐
Alfred Hitchcock	☐
David Lean	☐

19 Elizabeth Taylor

Conrad Hilton	☐
Ray Milland	☐
Robert Preston	☐

20 Bruce Willis

Glenn Close	☐
Madonna	☐
Demi Moore	☐

ANSWERS
Pot Luck

1 | Israel

2 | Boxing

3 | Sir Isaac Newton

4 | Julius Caesar

5 | Peter

6 | A brain

7 | Joan Collins

8 | TS Eliot

9 | Alistair MacLean

10 | Alfred Hitchcock

Pot Luck

Fill in the answers to the following general knowledge questions about famous people:

1 David Ben-Gurion became prime minister of which new state created in 1948?

2 In which sport did Henry Cooper become famous?

3 Who wrote a book about the forces and rules of motion called *Principia Mathematica*?

4 Who was warned by a soothsayer to 'beware the Ides of March', but was later murdered?

5 In the Bible, which of the disciples tried to walk on water?

6 In the film *The Wizard of Oz*, what did the straw man want?

7 Which actress played the role of Alexis in the TV series *Dynasty*?

8 Which poet wrote *Old Possum's Book of Practical Cats*?

9 Who wrote the novel *The Guns of Navarone*?

10 Who directed the films *The Birds*, *North by Northwest* and *Psycho*?

ANSWERS

11 Desmond Tutu

12 Romantic novels

13 Mother Teresa

14 Paul Hogan

15 Nelson Mandela

16 They uncovered the Watergate affair

17 Harold Macmillan

18 Alice

19 Mime

20 Richard Murdoch

11 In 1986, who became the Archbishop of Cape Town?

12 What kind of books are written by Barbara Cartland?

13 Which Roman Catholic nun became famous for her work among the poor of Calcutta?

14 Who played Crocodile Dundee in the film of the same name?

15 Which famous South African leader was released from prison in February 1990?

16 What did the American journalists Carl Bernstein and Bob Woodward do in 1973 to make headlines?

17 Which British prime minister was nicknamed 'Supermac'?

18 In the poem, with whom did Christopher Robin visit Buckingham Palace?

19 What is Marcel Marceau famous for in the theatre?

20 Who starred in the BBC radio show *Much Binding in the Marsh* with Kenneth Horne?

ANSWERS

Who Played Who?

1 Jessica Tandy

2 Christopher Reeve

3 Alec Guinness

4 Liza Minnelli

5 Gene Hackman

6 Walter Matthau

7 Anne Bancroft

8 Audrey Hepburn

9 Sidney Poitier

10 Elizabeth Taylor

QUESTIONS

Who Played Who?

 Choose from the alternatives given which actor played the part named in each film:

1 Miss Daisy in *Driving Miss Daisy*

Jessica Tandy	☐
Peggy Ashcroft	☐
Merle Oberon	☐

2 Clark Kent in *Superman*

Tom Cruise	☐
Mel Gibson	☐
Christopher Reeve	☐

3 Ben Kenobi in *Star Wars*

James Mason	☐
Alec Guinness	☐
Sean Connery	☐

4 Sally Bowles in *Cabaret*

Mia Farrow	☐
Liza Minnelli	☐
Meryl Streep	☐

5 'Popeye' Doyle in *The French Connection*

Gene Hackman	☐
Clint Eastwood	☐
Robert Mitchum	☐

6 Oscar Madison in *The Odd Couple*

Stephen Boyd	☐
Walter Matthau	☐
Tony Curtis	☐

7 Mrs Robinson in *The Graduate*

Anne Bancroft	☐
Jane Fonda	☐
Jean Simmons	☐

8 Eliza Dolittle in *My Fair Lady*

Audrey Hepburn	☐
Julie Andrews	☐
Barbra Streisand	☐

9 Virgil Tibbs in *In the Heat of The Night*

Eddie Murphy	☐
Sidney Poitier	☐
Danny Glover	☐

10 Cleopatra in *Cleopatra*

Elizabeth Taylor	☐
Jane Russell	☐
Maggie Smith	☐

ANSWERS

11 | Paul Newman

12 | Yul Brynner

13 | Anthony Perkins

14 | Frank Sinatra

15 | Doris Day

16 | Gary Cooper

17 | Michael Caine

18 | Marlon Brando

19 | Ben Kingsley

20 | Sean Connery

11 Fast Eddie Felson in *The Hustler*

Robert Redford	☐
Paul Newman	☐
Dustin Hoffman	☐

12 The King of Siam in *The King and I*

Richard Burton	☐
Telly Savalas	☐
Yul Brynner	☐

13 Norman Bates in *Psycho*

Michael Douglas	☐
Anthony Perkins	☐
Oliver Reed	☐

14 Maggio in *From Here to Eternity*

Frank Sinatra	☐
Montgomery Clift	☐
Marlon Brando	☐

15 Calamity Jane in *Calamity Jane*

Debbie Reynolds	☐
Doris Day	☐
Susan Haywood	☐

16 Marshall Will Kane in *High Noon*

John Wayne	☐
Alan Ladd	☐
Gary Cooper	☐

17 Harry Palmer in *The Ipcress File*

Michael Caine	☐
Laurence Harvey	☐
Peter O'Toole	☐

18 Don Corleone in *The Godfather*

Orson Welles	☐
Marlon Brando	☐
Robert Shaw	☐

19 Gandhi in *Gandhi*

Ben Kingsley	☐
Robert De Niro	☐
John Hurt	☐

20 James Bond in *Goldfinger*

Roger Moore	☐
Sean Connery	☐
Pierce Brosnan	☐

ANSWERS

20th-Century Women

1 Brigitte Bardot

2 Opera

3 Indira Gandhi

4 Glenda Jackson

5 Anita Roddick

6 Edith Piaf

7 She wrote poetry and novels

8 Beatrix Potter

9 Clothes

10 She sang opera

20th-Century Women

Fill in the answers to the following general knowledge questions about famous people:

1 Which French film star and sex symbol married Roger Vadim and in her later years has campaigned on behalf of animal rights?

2 In which of the arts did Maria Callas become famous?

3 Who was India's first woman prime minister?

4 Which British actress was awarded two Oscars and later, in 1992, became a Labour MP?

5 Whose concern for the environment and the body led her to create 'The Body Shop'?

6 Which French singer was well known for singing 'Je Ne Regrette Rien' and was affectionately known as 'the Little Sparrow'?

7 What did Sylvia Plath do to become well known?

8 Which children's writer, who lived in the Lake District, created the character Peter Rabbit?

9 What did Mary Quant design that brought her both success and public attention in the 1950s and 1960s?

10 What did the Australian Joan Sutherland do to become world famous?

11	**Shirley Temple**
12	**Women's rights (in particular, the right to vote)**
13	**Grace Kelly**
14	**Cello**
15	**Gymnastics**
16	**Marie Stopes**
17	**Anne Frank**
18	**Labour**
19	**Mary Whitehouse**
20	**Madonna**

QUESTIONS

11 Which American child star in later life became the US representative at the United Nations, appointed by President Nixon?

12 Emmeline Pankhurst vigorously campaigned for what cause?

13 Which American film star married Prince Rainier III of Monaco?

14 What musical instrument did Jacqueline du Pré become famous for playing?

15 In which Olympic sport did Olga Korbut take part?

16 Who founded the first birth control clinic in Britain?

17 Whose diary was published in 1947 and told the story of how she and her family went into hiding to escape Nazi persecution?

18 To which political party did Barbara Castle belong?

19 Which famous schoolteacher and broadcaster became famous for her campaign to clean up the media, in particular television?

20 Who had hits with the songs 'Like a Virgin' and 'Lucky Star'?

Section 10

Assorted Surnames

1   **Henrik Ibsen**

2   **Frank Ifield**

3   **Vidkun Quisling**

4   **Fred Quimby**

5   **Peter Ustinov**

6   **Jules Verne**

7   **Rudolph Valentino**

8   **Frank Winfield Woolworth**

9   **Andy Warhol**

10   **Richard Wagner**

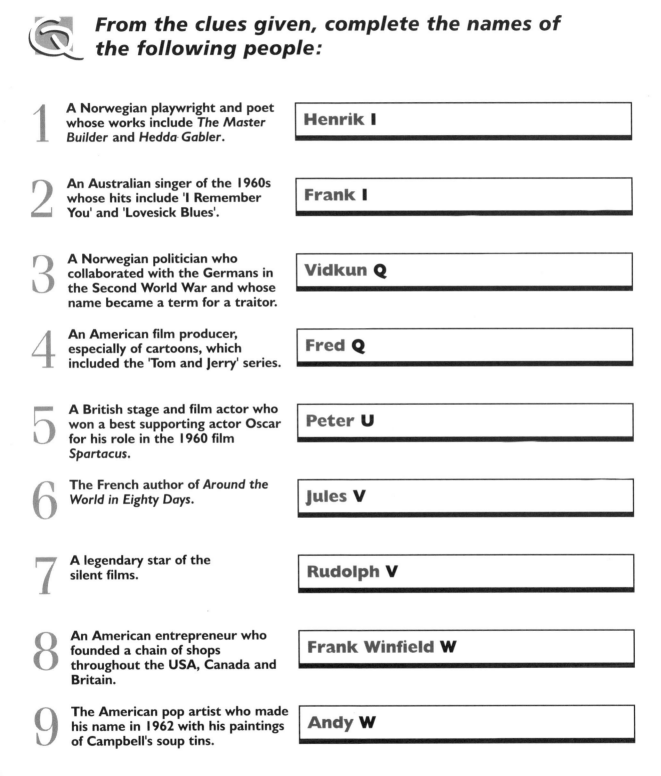

QUESTIONS

Assorted Surnames

From the clues given, complete the names of the following people:

1 A Norwegian playwright and poet whose works include *The Master Builder* and *Hedda Gabler*.

Henrik I

2 An Australian singer of the 1960s whose hits include 'I Remember You' and 'Lovesick Blues'.

Frank I

3 A Norwegian politician who collaborated with the Germans in the Second World War and whose name became a term for a traitor.

Vidkun Q

4 An American film producer, especially of cartoons, which included the 'Tom and Jerry' series.

Fred Q

5 A British stage and film actor who won a best supporting actor Oscar for his role in the 1960 film *Spartacus*.

Peter U

6 The French author of *Around the World in Eighty Days*.

Jules V

7 A legendary star of the silent films.

Rudolph V

8 An American entrepreneur who founded a chain of shops throughout the USA, Canada and Britain.

Frank Winfield W

9 The American pop artist who made his name in 1962 with his paintings of Campbell's soup tins.

Andy W

10 The German composer of the operas *Lohengrin* and *Tannhäuser*.

Richard W

11 John Wayne

12 John Wesley

13 Stevie Wonder

14 George Washington

15 St Francis Xavier

16 Linus Yale

17 Boris Yeltsin

18 Cole Younger

19 Susannah York

20 Emile Zola

11 The legendary American film actor famous for his lead roles in classic westerns.

> John **W**

12 The founder of the Methodist Church.

> John **W**

13 An American singer whose hits include 'For Once in My Life' and 'Happy Birthday'.

> Stevie **W**

14 The first president of the USA.

> George **W**

15 A Spanish Jesuit missionary who established Christian missions in Goa and Japan in the 16th century.

> St Francis **X**

16 An American inventor who set up business in Massachusetts to make locks named after him.

> Linus **Y**

17 He became Soviet president after Mikhail Gorbachev.

> Boris **Y**

18 A member of Jesse James's gang of outlaws.

> Cole **Y**

19 A British actress whose films include *Oh What a Lovely War* and *A Man for All Seasons*.

> Susannah **Y**

20 A French author whose works include *Germinal* and *Three Cities*.

> Emile **Z**

1   Vincent van Gogh

2   Andy Warhol

3   JMW Turner

4   Henri de Toulouse Lautrec

5   Graham Sutherland

6   Auguste Rodin

7   Claude Monet

8   LS Lowry

9   Leonardo da Vinci

10   David Hockney

QUESTIONS

Art and Artists

From the alternatives given, choose which artist painted the named painting:

1 'Landscape at St Remy'

Vincent van Gogh	☐
Paul Gauguin	☐
James Tissot	☐

2 'Marilyn'

LS Lowry	☐
Andy Warhol	☐
David Hockney	☐

3 'Snowstorm: Steamboat off a Harbour's Mouth'

JMW Turner	☐
Pierre Auguste Renoir	☐
Jackson Pollock	☐

4 'Dance at the Moulin Rouge'

Rembrandt	☐
Peter Paul Rubens	☐
Henri de Toulouse Lautrec	☐

5 'Portrait of Somerset Maugham'

Graham Sutherland	☐
William Hogarth	☐
William Blake	☐

6 'The Kiss'

Raphael	☐
Vincent van Gogh	☐
Auguste Rodin	☐

7 'Waterlily Pond'

Michelangelo	☐
JMW Turner	☐
Claude Monet	☐

8 'Coming From the Mill'

John Constable	☐
LS Lowry	☐
Salvador Dali	☐

9 'Mona Lisa'

Leonardo da Vinci	☐
Thomas Gainsborough	☐
Edouard Manet	☐

10 'A Bigger Splash'

LS Lowry	☐
David Hockney	☐
Graham Sutherland	☐

ANSWERS

11 Vincent van Gogh

12 Salvador Dali

13 John Constable

14 Paul Cezanne

15 Edouard Manet

16 JMW Turner

17 Pierre Auguste Renoir

18 Rembrandt

19 Michelangelo

20 Jean Baptiste Camille Corot

11 'Sunflowers'

Auguste Rodin ☐

Vincent van Gogh ☐

Henri de Toulouse Lautrec ☐

12 'Sleep'

Jackson Pollock ☐

Salvador Dali ☐

Henri Matisse ☐

13 'The Lock'

John Constable ☐

Paul Gauguin ☐

JMW Turner ☐

14 'Monte Sainte-Victoire'

Paul Cezanne ☐

Michelangelo ☐

Leonardo da Vinci ☐

15 'Music in the Tuileries Gardens'

Henry Matisse ☐

Edouard Manet ☐

Pierre August Renoir ☐

16 'The Fighting 'Temeraire"

Henri Matisse ☐

JMW Turner ☐

Sir Anthony Van Dyck ☐

17 'A Bather'

Pierre Auguste Renoir ☐

Peter Paul Rubens ☐

Paul Gauguin ☐

18 'Balshazzar's Feast'

Leonardo da Vinci ☐

Vincent van Gogh ☐

Rembrandt ☐

19 'The Entombment'

Edouard Manet ☐

Michelangelo ☐

Henri Matisse ☐

20 'The Wood Gatherer'

Jean Baptiste Camille Corot ☐

Thomas Gainsborough ☐

Paul Cezanne ☐

ANSWERS
Pot Luck

1 Nicholas II

2 Henry Ford

3 St Helena

4 Robert the Bruce

5 Hairdressing

6 Deadwood

7 John Masefield

8 Samuel Morse

9 John F Kennedy

10 Richard Branson

Pot Luck

Fill in the answers to the following general knowledge questions about famous people:

1 Who was the last Tsar of Russia?

2 Who introduced the Model T car in 1903?

3 Napoleon Bonaparte died on which island?

4 Which Scottish king defeated the English at Bannockburn?

5 Vidal Sassoon became a leading exponent in which business?

6 Jack McCall shot Wild Bill Hickok in 1876 in which town?

7 Which poet wrote 'I must go down to the sea again'?

8 Who developed the electric telegraph system and the code named after him?

9 Which American president was a torpedo boat commander in the Second World War?

10 Who founded the Virgin group of companies?

11 | Janet Leigh

12 | George Bush

13 | Penguin Books

14 | Robert Louis Stevenson

15 | Cecil B de Mille

16 | HMS *Bounty*

17 | Crime

18 | Six

19 | Julius Caesar

20 | Cricket

QUESTIONS

11 Jamie Lee Curtis is the daughter of which famous actress?

12 Which American president said "Read my lips: no new taxes"?

13 Sir Allen Lane founded which famous publishing company?

14 The *Weir of Hermiston* was the last, unfinished, novel of which Scottish author?

15 Which American film maker was famous for his biblical epics, including *Samson and Delilah* and *The Ten Commandments*?

16 Captain Bligh lost command of which ship after a famous mutiny?

17 What sort of books did the novelist Edgar Wallace write?

18 How many kings named George have sat on the British throne?

19 Who wrote 'Veni, vidi, vici' after invading England?

20 Which sport did Sir Donald Bradman play?

Countries of Birth

1 **Denmark**

2 **Britain**

3 **New Zealand**

4 **Nicaragua**

5 **Britain**

6 **Switzerland**

7 **Mexico**

8 **Poland**

9 **Britain**

10 **America**

QUESTIONS

Countries of Birth

From the three alternatives given, choose the country in which each of the following people was born:

1 Hans Christian Andersen

Holland	☐
Norway	☐
Denmark	☐

2 Charlie Chaplin

Britain	☐
America	☐
Canada	☐

3 Edmund Hillary

Australia	☐
New Zealand	☐
Britain	☐

4 Bianca Jagger

Nicaragua	☐
Mexico	☐
Honduras	☐

5 Bob Hope

America	☐
Canada	☐
Britain	☐

6 Carl Jung

Germany	☐
Switzerland	☐
Italy	☐

7 Anthony Quinn

Greece	☐
Spain	☐
Mexico	☐

8 Helena Rubenstein

Poland	☐
Hungary	☐
France	☐

9 David Hockney

America	☐
Australia	☐
Britain	☐

10 Eamon De Valera

Ireland	☐
Canada	☐
America	☐

11 Russia

12 Germany

13 Austria

14 Australia

15 Czechoslovakia

16 Poland

17 India

18 Russia

19 Italy

20 Iraq

QUESTIONS

11 Yul Brynner

Russia	☐
Mexico	☐
Bulgaria	☐

12 Henry Kissinger

South Africa	☐
Germany	☐
America	☐

13 Marie Antoinette

France	☐
Austria	☐
Luxembourg	☐

14 Rupert Murdoch

Canada	☐
Australia	☐
America	☐

15 Robert Maxwell

Czechoslovakia	☐
Poland	☐
Hungary	☐

16 David Ben-Gurion

Egypt	☐
Russia	☐
Poland	☐

17 Cliff Richard

India	☐
Kenya	☐
New Zealand	☐

18 Irving Berlin

Hungary	☐
Romania	☐
Russia	☐

19 Christopher Columbus

Spain	☐
Italy	☐
Portugal	☐

20 Charles & Maurice Saatchi

Iraq	☐
Saudi Arabi	☐
Iran	☐

1 | **Sean Connery**

2 | **George C Scott**

3 | **Frank Sinatra**

4 | **John McEnroe**

5 | **Rudyard Kipling**

6 | **Men's decathlon**

7 | **The Beatles**

8 | **Boxing (light heavyweight)**

9 | **Queen Victoria (63 years 7 months)**

10 | **Seven**

QUESTIONS

Winners

Fill in the answers to the following general knowledge questions about famous people:

1 Which former 'Mr Universe' competitor (1953) became a cult figure as James Bond?

2 Who refused his Oscar nomination for playing the part of General Patton in the film *Patton*?

3 Who received a Grammy Award for his recording of the hit song 'Strangers In The Night' in 1966?

4 Which tennis champion, known as 'the brat' because of his behaviour, won the men's singles championship at Wimbledon in 1981, 1983 & 1984?

5 Who won the Nobel prize for literature in 1907 for his *Jungle Book* and *Just So* stories?

6 Which world championship event did Daley Thompson win in 1983?

7 Whose top-selling single, 'I Want To Hold Your Hand', released in 1963, topped 13 million sales to make the top-selling British single in the UK?

8 In which sport did Freddie Mills become a world champion?

9 Who was Britain's longest reigning monarch?

10 How many gold medals did the American swimmer Mark Spitz win in the 1972 Olympics?

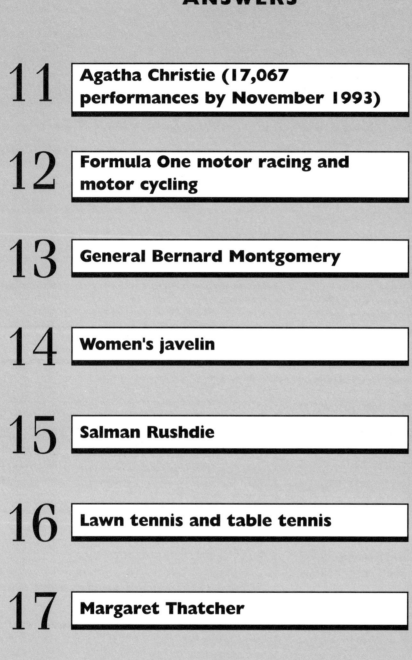

ANSWERS

11 Agatha Christie (17,067 performances by November 1993)

12 Formula One motor racing and motor cycling

13 General Bernard Montgomery

14 Women's javelin

15 Salman Rushdie

16 Lawn tennis and table tennis

17 Margaret Thatcher

18 Literature

19 Golf

20 Arnold Schwarzenegger

11 Who wrote the world's longest running play, *The Mousetrap*?

12 In which two sports did John Surtees become world champion?

13 Which British commander led the Eighth Army in the Second World War and defeated the German General Rommel?

14 In which athletics event did Fatima Whitbread win a world championship in 1987?

15 Who won the Booker prize for his novel *Midnight's Children* in 1981 and later received a death threat for another novel, *The Satanic Verses*?

16 In which two sports did Fred Perry become a champion?

17 Who has been Britain's longest serving prime minister this century?

18 For what did John Steinbeck win the Nobel Prize in 1962?

19 In which sport did the South African Gary Player become a champion?

20 Which former 'Mr Universe' starred in the films *Conan The Barbarian* and *Total Recall*?

Also Available from Speechmark ...

Speechmark publishes and distributes a wide range of creative resources providing exciting and appealing ideas for countless group activities. Listed below are just a few of these products – a full catalogue is available on request.

The Activity & Reminiscence Handbook

Hundreds of Ideas in 52 Weekly Sessions

Danny Walsh

This week-by-week guide provides a bumper book of original resource material for reminiscence and activities with older people for a whole year! Containing 52 selections of ideas and resource materials for each week of this year, this is an invaluable and easy to use resource relevant for both groups and individuals.

Pocket Quiz Books

Karen Hitchcow

These three convenient books provide thousands of themed quiz questions in a format that is easy to use with any group. They are suitable for all abilities and all kinds of groups, with answers printed alongside each question, making it easy for the group leader to preselect questions.

The Winslow Quiz Book

Robin Dynes

A form favourite for many years, the Quiz Book contains more than 2,000 questions categorised into 40 stimulating subjects. It is designed for those who use quizzes as a group activity and is aimed at adolescents and adults aloke, with questions realistically within the scope of the average person, covering topics such as cooking, geography, proverbs, sport and general knowledge.

Musical Quiz

Now available on CD, our popular musical quiz is more versatile, allowing you to play tracks in random order or easily repeat any track. There are eighty different melodies, played on a vaiety of instruments and covering songs from the 1930s onwards, including such favourites as 'Born Free', 'Catch a Falling Star', 'Delilah', 'Moon River' and 'The Last Waltz'.

Creative Games in Groupwork

Robin Dynes

Offering the opportunity to create a balanced programme, this well-organized and easy-to-use book contains scores of ideas for both indoor and outdoor games. Ideas include introductory and mixing exercises, games using gentle movement, exuberant games, puzzles and brain teasers, verbal games, pen and paper games and many, many more.

Memory Games for Groups

Robin Dynes

A wonderfully practical handbook featuring 80 adaptable and photocopiable games for use with older people, as well as ndividuals or groups of all ages. The games are designed to be made easier or more difficult to meet the needs of the individuals involved.

For further information please contact